The ASTD Trainer's Sourcebook:

DIVERSITY

Books in The ASTD Trainer's Sourcebook Series

The ASTD Trainer's Sourcebook:
DIVERSITY

Tina Rasmussen

McGraw-Hill, Inc.

New York   San Francisco   Washington D.C.   Auckland   Bogotá
Caracas   Lisbon   London   Madrid   Mexico City   Milan
Montreal   New Delhi   San Juan   Singapore
Sydney   Tokyo   Toronto

Library of Congress Catalog Card Number: 95-076449

5 6 7 8 9   MAL/MAL   6 5 4 3 2 1

ISBN 0-07-053438-1

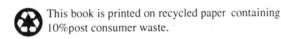

This book is printed on recycled paper containing 10%post consumer waste.

This book is printed on acid-free paper.

Sourcebook Team:

Co-Publishers:	Philip Ruppel, McGraw-Hill Training
	Nancy Olson, American Society for Training and Development
Acquisitions Editor:	Richard Narramore, McGraw-Hill Training
Editing Supervisor:	Paul R. Sobel, McGraw-Hill Book Group
Production Supervisor:	Pamela A. Pelton, McGraw-Hill Book Group
Series Advisor:	Richard L. Roe
Managing Editor:	Anne Coyle
Editor:	Charlene Ables
Image Formatting:	Claire Condra Arias, Ellipsys International Publications, Inc.

This book is dedicated to the people of Nestlé Beverage Company—

From the president to the receptionist,

From the East coast to the West—

Who have struggled in their day-to-day lives

To make the value for diversity

A reality.

Contents

Preface

I'd like to tell you how this series came about. As a long-time editor and resource person at Human Resources Development Publishing Company, I was frequently asked by trainers, facilitators, consultants, and instructors to provide them with training designs on a variety of topics. These customers wanted one-hour, half-day, and full-day programs on such topics as team-building, coaching, diversity, supervision, and sales. Along with the training designs, they required facilitator notes, participant handouts, flipchart ideas, games, activities, structured experiences, overhead transparencies, and instruments. But, that wasn't all. They wanted to be able to reproduce, customize, and adapt these materials to their particular needs—at no cost!

Later, as an independent editor, I shared these needs with Nancy Olson, the publisher at the American Society for Training and Development. Nancy mentioned that ASTD received many similar calls from facilitators who were looking for a basic library of reproducible training materials. Many of the classic training volumes, such as Jones and Pfeiffer's Handbook of Structured Experiences and Newstrom and Scannell's Games Trainers Play provided a variety of useful activities. However, they lacked training designs, handouts, overheads, and instruments—and, most importantly, they tended to be organized by method rather than by topic. You can guess the rest of the story: Welcome to The ASTD Trainer's Sourcebook.

This sourcebook is part of an open-ended series that covers the training topics most often found in many organizations. Instead of locking you into a prescribed "workbook mentality," this source-book will free you from having to buy more workbooks each time you present training. This volume contains everything you need— background information on the topic, facilitator notes, training designs, participant handouts, activities, instruments, flipcharts, overheads, and resources—and it's all reproducible! We welcome you to adapt it to your particular needs. Please photocopy. . . edit . . . add your name . . . add your client's name. Please don't tell us . . . it isn't necessary! Enjoy.

Richard L. Roe
ASTD Sourcebook Series Advisor

The ASTD Trainer's Sourcebook:

DIVERSITY

Chapter One:

Introduction

PICTURE THIS:

You get a call from a long-time associate and friend telling you she has the perfect career opportunity for you. You aren't looking for a new job, you're pretty happy where you are. But the offer is a good career move and financial opportunity. Besides, you've always wanted to live in San Francisco. So you take it. The company pays for your move, you have a few weeks off to settle in, and life is looking pretty rosy.

Your first day of work goes smoothly with lots of introductions, and a nice new office with your name already on the door. You go home, telling significant others that you think this will work out fine. You're feeling pretty pleased with yourself.

By day two you're starting to feel a little more confident, a little more at home. But your friend/boss seems tense. Then—**Wham!** She tells you she's resigned to take a position at another company. **Boom!** She tells you that instead of doing the project you were hired for, you are now going to be responsible for launching the corporate diversity effort she had just begun. **Bang!** You've never even contemplated working on a diversity effort, and you know nothing about it.

Some Good News and Some Bad News

This is how I became involved in the diversity intervention upon which the materials in the book are based. The good news is that I learned a lot, I've seen tremendous progress in the area of diversity, and the work has been tremendously rewarding.

The bad news is that I felt a lot of stress initially because there were no appropriate diversity materials available. In previewing numerous off-the-shelf programs, I found that most programs focused to some extent on "culture," or were basically just repackaged affirmative action training. By focusing on "what women do" or "how African-Americans think," they actually served to *reinforce* stereotypes rather than overcome them. Because of this, I decided to create my own approach to diversity, focusing on its benefit to *all* employees and positioning diversity as a bottom-line issue which taps into the new American workplace and consumer base.

Writing this book has been rewarding, because it gives me the opportunity to spare others from my experience. So congratulations—you don't need to repeat my story! By purchasing this book, you have saved yourself a lot of time, effort, and maybe a few gray hairs as well.

This book incorporates leading-edge thinking in the field of diversity. More importantly, the materials have also been tested and used with *non*-experts—regular executives, middle managers, and frontline employees who are trying to make sense of and be productive in this new workplace. Often, theories look good on paper, but when we try to implement them with real people they fall flat. You can rest assured that people at all levels, from all different professions and organizational areas have tested out these materials. Their perceptions about the key business issues we face today and how diversity impacts them have been incorporated to ground this book in the real world, as well as to make it theoretically sound. I know you'll find this book to be a practical resource as well, and wish you much success in your diversity efforts.

This chapter of *The ASTD Trainer's Sourcebook: Diversity* contains an overview of the topic of diversity, including its major issues and controversies. It also presents the philosophical viewpoint embodied in this book.

This chapter contains four segments:

- Background on Diversity: Issues and Philosophy
    - What Diversity Is *Not*
    - What Diversity *Is*
- Managing Diversity
    - Positioning Diversity for Maximum Impact
    - Legal Issues
    - Our Responsibility as Training Professionals
- Key Diversity Training Topics
- The Remainder of This Book

Background on Diversity: Issues and Philosophy

What do we mean when we use the term *diversity*? As with any hot topic, one can find hundreds of definitions, all from "experts" and all different from each other.

This book takes a strong view of the definition of diversity, which extends beyond the original definitions from ten or more years ago. We've learned a lot about diversity over the years, and people's thinking about what is effective has changed quite a bit. We did many things in the early years of the diversity movement which may have actually hurt our efforts. You can benefit from these years of experimentation and practice by adopting the more evolved philosophy of diversity, rather than the earlier, less effective one. (Complete descriptions of this book's philosophy are contained in Chapter 6.)

What Diversity Is *Not*

Because of all the early misconceptions about diversity, it may be easier to begin by defining what diversity is *not*.

Diversity is not just a buzz word

It's true that diversity is a hot topic. Organizations that do not have diversity efforts may even feel behind the times. But diversity is more than just a buzz word. It is not something that will *ever* go away. It is grounded in a powerful combination of the human rights movement and our increasingly diverse and global marketplace—both of which have consistently gained momentum for the last twenty years and show no signs of fading.

Read the statistics. Look around. Watch the news. Read a newspaper or magazine. Once we are confronted with the hard, cold statistics, it becomes apparent that times have changed more rapidly than our perception of them—and they have changed forever. The individuals and organizations who will succeed in years to come are those who turn these changes into an advantage, not those who ignore them and hope they'll go away.

Diversity is not culture

A crucial mistake many people make in defining diversity is to equate it to culture. They think diversity training means teaching people about "what Asians are like," "characteristics of Hispanics," or "what women want." While this approach may appear sound on the surface, it is inherently flawed because all it does is *reinforce stereotypes*. Isn't that what we're trying to overcome by valuing diversity? This approach reinforces an "us versus them" mentality. It focuses on how we are different, rather than how we are alike. It is exclusive, not inclusive.

Valuing diversity extends far beyond culture to include all the primary and secondary dimensions diagrammed below. While most people have seen this diagram, the majority of diversity efforts do not tap into its full value. This model vividly demonstrates that we are all similar and different on an infinite number of dimensions. Culture is only one of them. It helps us relate to each other on the many characteristics which really make up who we are. By positioning diversity as something that applies to *everyone*, it becomes something that everyone can care about and support. Diversity trainers who speak to *all* their participants have learned to eliminate the word "culture" from their vocabulary. (See the Primary and Secondary Dimensions handout in Chapter 6, page 173.)

Primary and Secondary Dimensions of Diversity

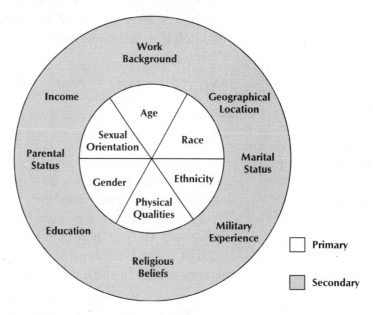

Loden and Rosener, *Workforce America!,* 1991

Diversity is not EEO affirmative action

In the early years of the diversity movement (and even today to some extent) people had a tendency to assume diversity was just a repackaging of EEO and affirmative action—that it was mainly about "quota filling." (See the History of Diversity and Approaches to Diversity handouts in Chapter 6, pages 176 and 178.) This is a detrimental and divisive view. While EEO and affirmative action were necessary steps and had their place in the evolution of the movement, they are distinctly different from valuing diversity. First, they are laws imposed on people, which creates an adversarial environment. Second, people interpret them to mean less qualified people should be given jobs, over more qualified traditional employees. The insinuation is that we have to help protected classes because they are not really qualified enough to succeed based on their own merits. This only adds to the conflict and reinforces stereotypes.

Valuing diversity, on the other hand, says that people's differences are an asset rather than a burden to be tolerated. In valuing diversity, we acknowledge that we may have preconceived ideas that can blind us from seeing the value that nontraditional employees bring. Only the most qualified candidate is given the job; *but* we have to transcend our biases about what is "most qualified." An organization that emphasizes quota-filling as part of its diversity effort will undermine the true intent of valuing diversity.

Diversity is not an absence of standards

People sometimes believe that valuing diversity means "anything goes"; that we give up our standards for hiring and promoting people. In fact, diversity is the opposite of this. Because we are removing our preconceived ideas about who is qualified for a job, we must create clearer definitions of actual job requirements.

For true equality to happen, there needs to be a *lack* of focus on race, gender, and other differences, and an increased focus on a person's *capabilities* and on system adjustments that support diversity. Only this approach will create a process which is *naturally* equal for everyone.

Diversity is not "white male bashing"

To some, diversity symbolizes a more enlightened society, a reflection of our future as global citizens. To others, it breeds resentment. And why shouldn't it, if diversity means that less qualified people are going to get the best jobs? Sentiments like these become the sounding cry of *backlash*.

These two extreme views are at the heart of the issue of diversity—and why diversity efforts so often *fail*. Although well-intentioned, a focus on culture, race, and gender—and blaming the white male for past injustices—only intensifies separation between groups, rather than bringing them together to create a more productive workplace.

Understandably, the historical, homogeneous group of white male workers created the American workplace based on their own similar backgrounds, styles, perspectives, values, and beliefs. But it is now time for a change which takes into account everyone's needs. Even the needs of the original homogeneous group have changed.

Unfortunately, the people who created the system are often labeled "the bad guys" when the system needs updating. In effect, positioning diversity so one group must take blame for the past makes the ultimate goal—greater unity—impossible.

What Diversity *Is*

Now that we've fully explored the misconceptions about diversity and what it *isn't*, let's look at what diversity *is*. What's it all about?

Diversity is about demographics

The diversity movement first began with the Workforce 2000 report, a landmark study commissioned by the U.S. Department of Labor in the 1980s. Because the results were so dramatic, many employers took a "wait and see" attitude initially. But as the predictions started coming true, more and more companies decided to pay attention to the growing diversity of their workforce *and of their customer base*.

Now, no one can argue with the demographic changes occurring in the United States. In 1965, the average worker was a married white male, 29 years old, with fewer than twelve years of education and a wife and children at home. In contrast, in 1992, 52 percent of working adults were women, and 11 percent of the men were minorities, which means only *37 percent* of working adults were white males—and the percentage is decreasing! The bottom line is that the workplace is not the way it used to be, though it is *structured* as if it were. It is just good business to reexamine a situation in which 63 percent of the workforce may be less productive than they could be, because they work in an outdated system. (See the handout, Workplace Trends and Statistics on page 174 in Chapter 6 and the Diversity Statistics Quiz on page 251 in Chapter 8 for details.)

Diversity is about profitability

While affirmative action focused on eliminating discrimination, valuing diversity is a bottom-line issue about increasing productivity and profitability. In fact, valuing diversity is one of the few social issues in which the business community is actually leading the way. Why? Because it *is* profitable. It fosters teamwork. It helps organizations identify and meet the needs of their customers and consumers. The organizations that have understood and used their understanding of diversity in innovative ways have found themselves an advantage in the marketplace.

Recent research has repeatedly revealed the business benefits of diversity. (See the handout, Advantages of Diverse Groups on page 180 in Chapter 6.) In the 1992 book *The New Leaders* by Ann Morrison, twelve companies were selected as models of diversity. Of these, eleven were later found to be included in *Fortune* magazine's list of most admired companies, and three won the Malcolm Baldridge Award for quality. An article in *Executive Excellence* magazine cites several studies, one by social psychologist Irving Janis who demonstrated that diverse groups make sounder decisions then homogeneous groups. In another study by the Goodmeasure consulting group headed by well-known management expert Rosabeth

Moss Kanter, research indicated that differences in perspectives and assumptions were one of the most important factors for team success. More innovative companies tended to have more women and minorities, and were also more financially successful.

Astute diversity proponents have realized that they need to draw upon this research more, to demonstrate that diversity is a *business* issue, not just a "moral" one. Without this link, it is difficult to gain support from senior management or a wide base of employees who may not otherwise see direct benefits of diversity.

Diversity is about values

Having said that diversity is a business issue, we must also affirm that it relates to people's values. Although people are sometimes more comfortable keeping this an impersonal issue—"strictly business"—diversity has to do with human rights, civil rights, and people's deeply held beliefs. It forces people to question thirty, forty, fifty or more years of social conditioning they have been subjected to since they were born. For some people, diversity is even related to their religious beliefs. How do we balance people's right to their personal values with the organization's right to create a productive workplace? Delicately, tactfully, respectfully, and also firmly, openly, persistently. We *admit* that valuing diversity is a personal decision; we *focus on* diversity as a business decision.

Diversity is about behavior

One tool for redirecting the values aspect of diversity to the business emphasis is to focus on diversity as a behavior. Regardless of our personal beliefs, our organizations expect us to work in the most productive possible manner, and valuing diversity is much more productive than *not* valuing it. The difficulty is: Once people leave a workshop, how do we keep up their motivation if they don't hold diversity as a value? This is where motivation comes in (to be discussed later in this chapter and in Chapter 2). As trainers, what's important for us to remember is this: It's not the workshop that's important, it's what people *do* afterward that counts.

Diversity is a long-term process

Because of the difficulties just stated, and because diversity is a large-scale change effort that extends far beyond training, diversity must be viewed as a long-term process. If an organization believes diversity can be addressed with a quick fix, or by simply putting people through workshops, it is likely to be disappointed. However, organizations that make a long-term commitment to a comprehensive strategy which includes training will not be disappointed and can see lasting benefits.

Diversity is a seed that you, as a diversity trainer and change agent, can plant and nurture to bloom in a few years—maybe as many as five to ten. Your chances of nurturing a healthy flower are dependent in large part upon your ability to generate ownership for the effort by everyone in the organization, from the president to the receptionist. Diversity must be woven into all other business efforts, such as the vision, values, plans, budgets, TQM, reengineering, and so on. Plant the seeds today, and plant as many as you can, but you need to keep nurturing them—and you *will* see blooms in a few years.

Diversity defined

To encompass all the ideas we have discussed in this chapter, we will define diversity as:

> The mosaic of people who bring a variety of backgrounds, styles, perspectives, values, and beliefs as assets to the groups and organizations with which they interact.

This definition has three notable points. First, it describes diversity as a *mosaic*, which is different from the traditional U.S. melting pot. A mosaic enables people to retain their individuality while contributing to a collectively larger picture. Second, this definition of diversity applies to and *includes everyone*; it is not exclusionary. According to this definition, we are *all* diverse. Finally, this definition describes diversity as an *asset,* as something desirable and beneficial.

The Platinum Rule

A key component of "what diversity is" revolves around use of The Platinum Rule, which is an extension of The Golden Rule. The Platinum Rule is this: **Treat others as *they* want to be treated**.

The Platinum Rule is the cornerstone of diversity behavior as presented in this book, because it demonstrates respect and honoring of our differences by assuming others may want to be treated differently than we do. It also implies that we need to *ask* others what *they* want, and *tell* others what *we* want. Using The Platinum Rule takes diversity beyond culture, and ensures that everyone is included and everyone wins.

Diversity is a celebration

Finally, valuing diversity is a celebration of our humanity, of our individual uniqueness as well as our group commonality. It gives us permission to be appreciated for who we are, and to laugh at ourselves for all our strengths and weaknesses. At its best, valuing diversity is openness, fun, and joy in discovering how we can join together—with all our complementary human characteristics—to create more as a united team than any one of us can on our own.

Managing Diversity

Valuing diversity is also about infrastructures, which leads us to the distinct concept of *managing* diversity. Managing diversity is different from valuing diversity because it addresses the organizational processes which can reinforce—or hinder—the ability to create an environment that values diversity. Infrastructures include things like hiring, promotion, communication, and power allocation.

A person's role as a manager brings with it many additional elements beyond the scope of valuing diversity. Managers are *absolutely critical* to an organization's ability to successfully create an environment which values diversity. They set the tone and are the role models for their teams. When the workshops are over, people will look to *them* to see whether diversity is a real value in the organization, or whether it is just a fad to be forgotten in a few months.

Positioning Diversity for Maximum Impact

As a diversity trainer and change agent, you can take two important actions to position your diversity effort for maximum impact: customizing it for your organization, and continually answering your participants' (and the organization's) question, "what's in it for me?"

The power of customization

With an organizational change effort such as diversity, it is not enough to just take an off-the-shelf diversity program such as this and use it "as is" without first finding out about your organization's specific needs, as well as potential obstacles. Why is this? Why can't we just give people a tried-and-true workshop? Because valuing diversity is not simply a *skill*, such as selling or communicating. Valuing diversity hits at the heart of people's long-held values and beliefs. Skills and observable behavior are part of the picture; but valuing diversity often strikes deeper, at how people were raised and how they see the world. People need to know how it affects their particular organization (and themselves as individuals) to be motivated to take action.

Fortunately, most companies have some core values and business needs already in place that can help to lay a foundation upon which to build a successful diversity effort. The trick is finding those needs and linking them to the change process.

Rest assured that this sourcebook provides you with tools for doing this. Chapter 2, Workshop Preparation, describes this process further. (Also, see the organizational instruments in Chapter 8 and the handout on page 169 in Chapter 6, Our Organization's Value for Diversity.) Your diversity effort will have maximum impact if you determine what specific diversity issues apply in your organization's situation, and focus the effort on those issues and the related benefits. The more precisely you can identify your organization's specific needs and issues, and the more closely you can link your organization's goals with the diversity effort, the more likely you are to generate commitment and enthusiasm. (For additional information, see the author's chapter in the ASTD book, *In Action: Conducting Needs Assessment*. This is an excellent resource on how to target and customize your own diversity effort using the instruments found in this sourcebook. A full description is in the Appendix. To order, call ASTD at 703-683-8100.)

"What's in it for me?"

Once you have determined "What's in it for the organization?" you need to determine the potential benefits for people *as individuals* in valuing diversity. This needs to extend beyond "The organization says you should," because that is a weak motivation for a large change such as this.

People sometimes are threatened by the ideas discussed in workshops on valuing diversity, more so than in workshops on communication or other skills-oriented topics. The world's rapid movement toward diversity and away from homogeneity has turned the traditional power structures on their ear. Often, people hope these changes will just go away, and their resistance can be strong. Who can blame people? Change is difficult, and it may seem easier to ignore it.

The days when *anyone* in America can count on working with or selling to customers who are just like them are over—for good. We are *all* caught in a tide which is moving toward increasing diversity. The people who will excel in five or ten years will be skilled at working with a *variety* of people, not just people who are like themselves. Whether our primary contacts are with people in other departments, our managers, people who report to us, or customers—we *need* those people if we're going to be successful. If we can't build productive relationships with them, our success will be limited.

You will have an opportunity in the next chapter, as part of your preparation, to think more about positioning diversity—both within the organization and with individuals—in ways which will help to increase motivation and maximize the impact of your diversity effort and training.

Legal Issues

Because diversity is so close to people's identities and values, it can be a volatile topic. In addition, despite the fact that valuing diversity aims to transcend the limitations of affirmative action, laws are still in effect which impact diversity efforts. Cases have been brought and won based on what was said in supposedly confidential training sessions, or written on flipcharts to record workshop discussions.

Trainers must be sensitive to legal implications and how their actions may be interpreted by workshop participants. Diversity trainers should *never* use a confrontational, harassing approach. Not only is it questionable legally, it is not an effective adult learning technique.

Written information must also be handled carefully. Flipcharts should never state that stereotypes or other potentially damaging statements are present or condoned in your organization. Trainers should always destroy written materials with potentially damaging statements by the end of the workshop. And most importantly, trainers should remain neutral and keep discussions focused on diversity as a bottom-line productivity issue rather than a discussion of the merits or tendencies of any particular demographic group.

This book does not provide legal advice. Ultimately, the facilitation of your diversity workshop is your decision and is under your control. It is an important responsibility. You may want to have your organization's legal department review your diversity training plan to ensure that they are comfortable with it before you begin implementing it.

Our Responsibility as Training Professionals

As you can see, diversity efforts are often more complex than straightforward training interventions. This book will help you handle this complexity, by being sensitive to and strategic about the training itself as well as the supporting efforts.

As trainers, we have a responsibility to take diversity to a new level of enlightenment and potential unity for everyone in the workplace. While we do need to keep legal issues in mind, simply repackaging our old EEO and affirmative action programs is not only less effective, but is a disservice to our organizations and our learners.

Viewing diversity beyond culture makes it a win for everyone. It becomes valuable for traditional employees because it prepares them with skills needed for the year 2000, and gives them the freedom to break out of stereotypes which may have influenced them unwillingly for years. It also gives nontraditional employees a chance to participate in the workplace on a level playing field. It's up to all of us, as individuals and as training professionals, to help create a new workplace which equally values *everyone*.

Key Diversity Training Topics

Diversity consists of several key topics. These are important for trainers to be aware of in conducting the workshops in this sourcebook. This chapter touches upon all of them. To learn more about these topics, read the handouts in Chapter 6, which are on the following topics:

- Diversity Definitions and Terms

- Primary and Secondary Dimensions of Diversity

- Workplace Trends and Statistics

- The History of Diversity

- Approaches to Diversity

- Advantages of Diverse Groups

- How We Form Perceptions

- Stereotyping

- Prejudice

- Behavior Basics

- Collusion

- The Platinum Rule

- Managing Diversity Versus Traditional Management

- How Managers Set a Tone for Valuing Diversity

- Diversity Employment Issues for Managers

- Team Guidelines and Communication for Managers

As you read the handouts, you will notice that the topics build in a coherent progression which follows the sequence of the workshop guides and activities. Many of the topics are linked, and build on and reference each other for a smooth flow. It is helpful for workshop participants to refer back and forth between the concepts, in order to build increasing credibility and grounding for people's commitment to taking action.

The Remainder of This Book

The remainder of this book contains three types of chapters, followed by an informative appendix and comprehensive index.

Chapter 2   **Workshop Preparation**

This chapter helps you understand how to use this book to prepare for a diversity change effort and workshop. It is a practical "how to" guide, including your role as a trainer, use of Chapters 3 through 9, logistics, and references for further reading.

Chapters 3 - 5   **Workshop Guides**

These chapters contain detailed guides for one-day, half-day, and one-hour workshops. They contain all the information you need to conduct a diversity workshop. They bring together the workshop materials and content in a meaningful, coherent instructional design.

Chapters 6 - 9   **Workshop Materials, Content**

These chapters contain the handouts, activities, assessments, and overheads you will use in your diversity workshops. They are brought together for you in the previous workshop guide chapters. You may also use the materials in these chapters to create your own workshop.

Appendix   **Recommended Reading**

This contains recommended resources for your own continued learning and for possible use in your workshop. It is an annotated bibliography of the author's "top ten" favorite resources.

Workshop Preparation

This chapter of *The ASTD Trainer's Sourcebook: Diversity* contains information you will need to prepare for your diversity workshop. It describes how to customize your diversity effort for your own organization's needs, including how to use organizational instruments and how to coach executives. It reviews facilitation tips as applied specifically to diversity training. It reviews how to use the diversity workshop guides and pull materials from the handout, activity, instrument, and overhead chapters. It also provides assistance with logistics such as pre-workshop memos, materials preparation, and room setup.

CHAPTER OVERVIEW

This chapter contains four segments:

- Effectively Facilitating a Diversity Change Effort
- Preparing for a Diversity Workshop
- Pre-workshop Communication and Marketing
- Preparing Facilities, Equipment, and Supplies

Workshop Preparation Outline

Effectively Facilitating a Diversity Change Effort

- Diversity Training in an Organizational Change Context
- How Individual Change Occurs
- Effective Roles
- Adult Learning Principles Applied to Diversity
- Facilitation Skills
- Who Should Facilitate Diversity Training?

Preparing for a Diversity Workshop

- Preparation Steps
- Contents of This Book
- Group Size
- Timing
- Facilitation Format Descriptions

Pre-workshop Communication and Marketing

- Naming the Workshop
- Kickoff Announcements and Memos
- Diversity Celebrations
- Pre-work/Manual
- Voice Mail Reminder
- Individual Contact with Participants
- Officer Kickoff and Workshop Participation

Preparing Facilities, Equipment, and Supplies

- Diversity Workshop Materials Checklist
- Room Setup Diagrams
- Participant Roster
- Name Tents
- Diversity Workshop Certificate

Effectively Facilitating a Diversity Change Effort

Diversity Training in an Organizational Change

Context

Why do we do training? In a business environment, the ultimate goal is usually related to increasing individual and organizational productivity in pursuit of the organization's vision and goals. In the context of this sourcebook, the purpose of training is:

> To give participants the opportunity to gain knowledge, adopt attitudes, develop skills, and modify behaviors which contribute to the goals and objectives of the organization.

Training does not have the ability to *force* people to change. It is not a miracle cure, quick fix, or all-powerful solution to large-scale organizational needs. Often, people attempt to create organizational change by putting on a workshop and forcing everyone to sit through it, without any follow-up by managers or system-wide supports for the ideas and skills put forth in the training. Then, nothing changes and everyone says, "Training doesn't work," or "What a waste of time." In large part, they are correct, because training only occurs for 4 or 8 or 16 hours, while the normal operations of our work day bear down on us 40 or more hours a week, and 2,080 hours a year. This is why the organizational development efforts done in conjunction with training are at least as important as workshops themselves, even though they aren't as visible or as much of an "event."

The most critical aspect of any workshop is what people do *after* it. Do they leave the session with a genuine commitment to take action? When they try to do something differently, do they find that they had enough time in the workshop to develop the skills they need? Do their managers support their attempts and reward them, or do they tell them "That's not the way we do things around here?" The answers to these questions help predict the degree of success (or failure) of any training effort, as much as the trainer's level of skill in implementing the workshop. This is why the role of the trainer is really the role of change agent. Your role doesn't end when the workshop is over. It continues on, in coaching and reinforcing the behaviors of managers and employees on a daily basis, until the change has become a habitual part of life in the organization.

Training is an important piece of any organizational change effort. It can generate enthusiasm, build momentum, create synergy and, at its best, help people to have "ah ha!" moments of personal insight. It can help people break old, inefficient, ineffective patterns and move into new, more productive ways of doing business. But diversity training must be done as part of a comprehensive organizational development strategy if it is to have a long-term impact.

In this book, we will focus primarily on the training aspect of a diversity effort. However, it is important to first set the training in the larger context of organizational change, which is the ultimate goal of any diversity effort.

How individual change occurs

Especially with a topic such as diversity, which is so rooted in people's values, it is important to review how people learn and change. We will define *learning* as:

> The questioning of assumptions and/or the acquisition of knowledge and competencies to effect cognitive and/or behavioral change.

This definition implies that learning can only occur when the learner is receptive to questioning the status quo, and when the learner is in a position to acquire new ways of perceiving or doing something. To take this a step further, we can say that learning begins when the learner is *motivated* to learn. Motivation then becomes a prerequisite for learning. This leads us to a core principle of diversity training which diversity trainers need to remember at all times:

Learning is a voluntary activity

We cannot force someone to learn. If people can't answer the question, "What's in it for me to value diversity?" they will not put in the effort. They may sit through a diversity workshop, but no change will occur as a result.

This presents a dilemma for trainers who do mandatory diversity training because many of the participants may not be motivated to learn. However, the trainer also has a responsibility to attempt to effect organizational change, and many organizations choose to make their diversity training mandatory. How do we reconcile this? The effective, creative change agent takes steps to enhance the learner's motivation, rather than to authoritatively try and force people to change—which is futile anyway.

The first step then, is to answer the question, "What's in it for the learner to care about diversity?" Take a moment now to think about the participants in the sessions you'll be facilitating. What's in it for them to care? Incorporate this into all your actions and communications. Possibilities include:

- Our customer base is becoming more diverse.

- People who work well with a variety of others will be more valuable in their jobs.

- People who are not good at valuing diversity will become "dinosaurs"—like those who can't use computers.

- Valuing diversity supports the organization's culture and goals.

- Your manager expects you to value diversity.

- Diversity is quickly becoming part of our society.

- It's the right thing to do.

- Others?

Effective Roles

For most people, the idea of participating in training is reminiscent of time spent in elementary school, high school, or college. Many people have some anxiety and resentment about it. This is normal and to be expected, because as adults, people are not comfortable being in a situation in which they are viewed as deficient, dependent, needing to be "fixed," are going to be put on the spot, or are at the mercy of an authoritarian figure. Unfortunately, adult learning situations sometimes do this to adults, which only reinforces the negative preconceptions.

To dispel these notions and set the appropriate tone for the workshop, it is useful to understand and openly establish the roles everyone fulfills. However, the trainer must first understand and role model a belief in a true learning partnership between trainer and participants.

The trainer's role

The trainer's role is to:

- Model valuing diversity by respecting the contribution of all participants.

- Treat people as responsible adults who are capable of using new information to make their own decisions.

- Ensure that participants understand the concepts discussed.

- Help people relate what they learn to real life.

- Help people figure out how they feel about diversity and what they're going to do about it.

- Create an environment in which people feel comfortable expressing their views and stretching their comfort zones.

- Help the group find its own answers to questions and difficult issues.

- Maintain the group's productivity.

- Keep the group focused on relevant issues.

- Mediate disagreements and conflict.

The trainer's role is not to:

- Treat people as students who lack knowledge and are passively waiting for the teacher to fill them with knowledge.

- Preach or lecture.

- Maintain rigid control of the group.

- Fulfill the authoritarian role as experienced in school.

- Know every answer to every question.

The participants' role

A participant's role is to:

- Be prepared by completing the pre-work.

- Participate when he or she has something to share—both supporting and challenging.

- Respect other participants.

- Contribute positively to the productivity of the group.

A participant's role is *not* to:

- Expect the trainer to resolve all issues or concerns, or to produce miracle solutions.

- Think of the workshop as a vacation day.

- Revert to behavior exhibited in childhood as a student.

Management's role   Officers and managers also have a huge role in the success of a diversity effort. People will look to them to see if the commitment to diversity is real or just lip service.

It is the trainer's job to coach managers at all levels in fulfilling their role. You need to keep asking them to do things that role model their leadership. If participants say their managers don't "walk the talk," you need to feed this information back to management as well. In doing these things, you become a true change agent rather than just an instructor.

You can help managers by letting them know their role includes:

- Participating in the training themselves.

- Supporting the time people spend in training.

- Acknowledging they are still learning about managing diversity, and may need help doing it.

- Being open to hearing about obstacles.

- Seeking feedback from people who report to them about their skill level in managing diversity.

- Addressing obstacles to valuing diversity.

In coaching managers, remind them what's in it for them to focus on this issue. Help them see these benefits:

- Leaders who are good at this will be more in demand in the future.

- Their own credibility as leaders may be at stake.

- Their bosses and the organization expects them to do it.

- It supports the organization's goals.

- It has a positive impact on productivity.

- It can improve the group's creativity and decision making.

- Providing a workplace free of discrimination is required by law.

Adult Learning Principles Applied to Diversity

Effective adult learning is much different from the learning we experienced as children (which often was not very effective for children, either!) Below is a review of commonly accepted adult learning principles as they apply to diversity training.

Acknowledge people's experience as valuable

Most adults resent the idea of having to be "taught" something. Adults believe they already know a lot, and that what they know is valuable and important—and they're right! Because diversity is such a new area, people are often fairly open to learning about it. The trainer can help by acknowledging that people's previous experiences with diversity are valid.

Make it "real world"

Adults need to know the relevance of what they learn to real life. They don't care about theoretical, "ivory tower" diversity concepts they'll never use. It is crucial to keep linking diversity with the bottom line.

Make it interactive

Adults like to learn actively. They don't like to be lectured to. If they discover diversity "ah ha's" on their own, they embrace the concepts more readily. By using the interactive activities in this sourcebook, and asking questions about the pre-readings rather than lecturing, you will keep the session interactive.

Be a role model

Adults expect the trainer to role model valuing diversity, as both a continuous learner on the subject and as a diversity champion. If people see you contradicting a value for diversity, your credibility and that of the program will suffer dramatically. Get feedback from peers on your behavior, and continually keep improving your actions as a champion.

Less is more

We have a tendency to tell people every single thing they might need to know, just in case. This idea seems valid, but actually hurts learners. It overwhelms them with more information than they can absorb, and it doesn't distinguish between *need to know* and *nice to know*. To make the training effective, only tell people what they need to know about diversity.

Let people progress at their own pace and make mistakes

Another tendency we have is to "save" learners by answering their diversity questions for them. The most valuable portion of learning is *not* when the trainer is giving answers, but when learners get to *do* something, formulate their own answers, and receive feedback from others. This is especially true with diversity training, because some participants will be more attuned to valuing diversity than others. Let people struggle with their own feelings and those of other participants. The workshop is a laboratory for experimentation, not a factory for production.

It may be helpful to view your role in this way. Every learner is somewhere on a scale of 1 to 10 in valuing diversity. If you can help someone who is a 5 move to 6 or 7, you have succeeded. If you guide someone who is a 9 to 10, you have succeeded. Not everyone is going to get to 10 in your workshop. Give people permission to be 5's, so long as they are willing to consider moving up on the scale. Let participants who are 9's or 10's influence those who are 5's, rather than you having to do it every time.

Facilitation skills   It is tempting to focus a large amount of effort on techniques, presentation skills, appearance, logistics, etc. in becoming a good diversity trainer. While all these things are important, they are not at the heart of good diversity workshop facilitation. Good trainers possess a core of small but highly important qualities which outweigh all the others combined. These are:

- Integrity

- A sincere belief in the value of diversity

- An authentic attempt to role model diversity, even if not perfectly

- Professionalism

- Openness

- Respect and empathy for learners in their efforts to value diversity

- A genuine desire to help people make practical use of what they learn

- Enthusiasm

- Credibility

We've all heard the phrase, "Your actions speak so loudly I can't hear what you're saying." This is especially true of diversity trainers. Credibility can be difficult to define, and develops over time. You can use the following guidelines to help establish your own credibility. This includes your ability to:

☑ **Help participants identify with you**

☑ **Come across as nonthreatening**

☑ **Project a neutral position (no "ax to grind")**

☑ **Speak from experiences of having been on the outside**

☑ **Project that you represent legitimate power (of senior management)**

☑ **Gently challenge participants' comfort zones**

☑ **Talk bottom-line business language**

☑ **Disclose your experiences and struggles as an advocate of diversity**

Who Should Facilitate Diversity Training?

People often debate whether a traditional employee (often a white male, or even a white female) can effectively facilitate diversity training. While this debate is not generally resolved, because of the broader, more inclusive perspective on diversity taken in this book, *anyone* can be an effective diversity trainer—if they are willing to honestly assess their own biases *and* they genuinely believe in the value of diversity. Remember, we are all diverse on an infinite number of variables. The most important factor is being able to empathize with others who are "on the outside." If you are going to be a diversity trainer and have not had this experience, you may want to immerse yourself in a situation in which you are excluded. Consider spending time in a neighborhood or country with a different racial or language group or doing a group activity which is usually exclusively done by the other gender.

Any effective diversity trainer needs to meet the above criteria. These should be the primary guidelines in trainer selection. A white male who genuinely believes in diversity *can* be a strong trainer, because white male participants may identify more easily with him.

Co-facilitation is another option which can be very effective. Using two trainers with different dimensions of diversity enables participants to relate to a wider range of elements. For example, a combination of male/female, white person/person of color, older/younger, married/single, and so on provides a nice balance.

Preparing for a Diversity Workshop

As a diversity trainer, you will be on the leading edge of a hot business issue which will affect the workplace for many years to come. This is an excellent opportunity for you to facilitate a process which will provide value to you personally and to your future career, and to contribute to the effectiveness of your organization.

Preparation Steps

Preparing for a diversity workshop includes eight steps:

1. Customize for your organization

As discussed in the introduction, your first step is using the three organizational instruments in Chapter 8 (pages 244, 247, and 249) to ground the workshops in an organizational development context.

Your diversity effort will have a much greater impact if you complete these instruments so that you can target your effort on your organization's particular issues. For example, a corporate headquarters in San Francisco may have diversity issues focusing on a wide variety of ethnic groups, lifestyles, and sexual orientations.

A manufacturing facility in a small, mostly white midwestern town might find that their diversity issues focus on the four religious groups with which employees have an allegiance, or on two small towns nearby that have been feuding with each other for years. A sales organization may focus primarily on the entry of women into the workplace, or on its ongoing problems with manufacturing or operations. A distribution group might find its primary focus is on management/employee relations. The point is to determine which of the primary and secondary dimensions are most strongly affecting your particular situation.

You will then customize the handout, Our Organization's Value for Diversity (page 169), and your presentation to reflect your organization's unique needs and methods for addressing those needs.

By customizing your effort, and then building other infrastructures to facilitate ongoing change, you can have a lasting impact. (See the Appendix for information on the book, *Needs Assessment in HRD,* which contains a case study by the author on how to customize a diversity effort using the instruments in this sourcebook.

2. Master the topic

Review this workbook several times, including the introduction, preparation, workshop chapter, and all handouts, activities, overheads, instruments, and suggested videos. The handouts are especially useful in gaining an understanding of the topic. You can even memorize them for use in presentation/discussion segments.

You may also want to use the video "A Class Divided," which is optional, but recommended for the one-day and half-day formats. "A Class Divided" is a powerful and entertaining documentary, originally created by ABC, which provides a rich, real-life demonstration of how prejudice occurs and the tremendously damaging effects it can have. (Ordering information can be found in the workshop guides in Chapters 3 and 4, and in the Appendix.)

You will also benefit from reading additional books and articles on diversity. The Appendix at the end of this book contains additional references with descriptions. A good primer on the subject is Roosevelt Thomas' classic 1990 article from the *Harvard Business Review*, "From Affirmative Action to Affirming Diversity," or his 1991 book, *Beyond Race and Gender.* Loden and Rosener's 1991 book, *Workforce America!* is also excellent.

3. Internalize the concepts

Next, you need to reflect honestly on your own feelings, thoughts, and ideas on this topic. How do you feel about it? Why are you doing it? Be honest with yourself about your own background, biases, and areas for improvement. Obtain feedback from others on your diversity behavior. Accept that you are not 100 percent perfect and that you need to work on this just as your participants do. Create a few goals for yourself in improving your value for diversity.

You can also incorporate your personal stories into the workshop to build rapport with participants and demonstrate your own learning.

4. Determine the training design

Once you have read this entire book and analyzed your organization's needs, you can select the most appropriate training design, whether it is one-day, half-day, one-hour, or your own customization. Each chapter has tips on how to customize the training.

5. Build facilitation skills

If you are a new trainer, read other materials by ASTD on group facilitation. If you are experienced, brush up on developmental areas. Rate yourself, or have others rate you, on the criteria listed on the Reaction Sheet (Chapter 8, page 271). These criteria are excellent goals for any trainer to work toward.

6. Practice, with feedback

Practice, practice, practice—with feedback! Star athletes and performers practice rigorously before a big event, and trainers need to as well. But practice doesn't automatically make perfect. If we practice something ineffective over and over, all we develop is a bad habit. We need feedback to make sure our practice is worthwhile. To do this, record yourself on audio- or videotape. Rehearse with people you are comfortable with, who will give you honest feedback. And always use Reaction Sheets to obtain feedback from participants to help you to continue honing your skills.

7. Continuously improve your skills

Before each session, take some deep breaths or do something that relaxes you. Don't put too much pressure on yourself—remember that this is not a life-or-death situation. At breaks, ask the group how it's going and make adjustments throughout the day, rather than waiting until the end and it's too late. Evaluate your own skills after each session according to the Reaction Sheet criteria.

David Wallechinski's 1991 *Book of Lists* cites speaking before a group as number one of the "Ten Worst Human Fears (in the U.S.)." (Note that death is number seven.) Don't let this apply to you! Prepare yourself by taking the above steps, and don't expect perfection. We are all learners—that's what the training field is all about. Projecting a value for your own continuous learning will gain more credibility with your participants than feigned perfection.

8. Coach the change

Your role doesn't end when the workshop is over. You need to keep feeding information back to management, coaching managers on their role modeling, being a champion of changing infrastructures, and addressing diversity obstacles. For more information on trainers as organizational change agents, refer to ASTD's publications on organizational development.

Contents of This Book

Once you have read this chapter, you should choose a workshop length and then review the suggested materials in the appropriate diversity workshop chapter (either 3, 4, or 5). Each chapter contains a guide, agenda, and your actual words and actions in conducting a diversity workshop. The workshop chapters incorporate all the information you need to implement the training "as is"—or to customize it for your own needs. Workshop formats are available for one-day, half-day, and one-hour sessions. You can easily take the one-day or half-day sessions and break them down into shorter workshops as well.

The following chapters (6, 7, 8, and 9) contain the handouts, activities, instruments, and overheads which have been incorporated into the workshop chapters. Once you have chosen a workshop length, photocopy the individual handouts, activities, instruments, and overheads so you have a complete loose-leaf composite of your materials. It may also be helpful to photocopy the step-by-step training plan for the workshop you select, so that you can highlight segments and add your own notes.

Each workshop chapter has the following segments:

- **Overview and Objectives**

- **Workshop Agenda**

    – A brief overview of the day.

- **Materials Needed**

    – A checklist of everything you need to pull from other chapters.

    – Diagrams of the flipcharts you will need to prepare before the session, and use during the workshop.

    – Suggestions for modifying the workshop if you desire.

- **Training Plan**

    – A step-by-step description of everything the trainer says and does during the entire workshop, including questions to ask, answers to look for, and use of all materials.

Navigating the Training Plans

The training plans are the heart of each of the seminar and work-shop sessions—the glue that draws and holds everything else together. These training plans are set out in detail on a module-by-module basis, with an agenda, statements of purpose, and objectives for each module. We have attempted to make these training plans as easy to use and as complete as possible. A sample is shown on the facing page with annotations explained below. The icons are translated on page 30.

1. Each section within a module has a heading that includes a statement of purpose for the section and suggested timing.

2. Within each section, you will find one or more major activities. Each is marked by an icon and a descriptive heading.

3. Additionally, you will find a number of supporting activities—each marked with an icon and explained with a suggested action.

4. Suggested actions are shown in conjunction with supporting activities—with the appropriate action verb in *UPPERCASE BOLD ITALIC*.

5. Suggested comments accompany many of the suggested actions. While these comments are fully "scripted," it is not intended that you "parrot" these remarks—but rather paraphrase the key thoughts in a way that is meaningful to you and the participants.

section heading

timing

icons

suggested comment

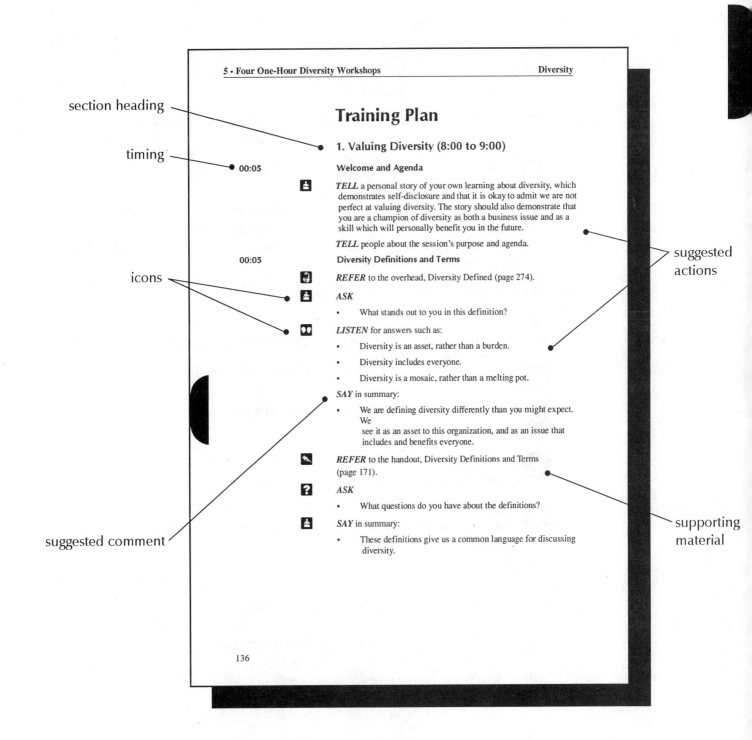

Training Plan

1. Valuing Diversity (8:00 to 9:00)

00:05 **Welcome and Agenda**

TELL a personal story of your own learning about diversity, which demonstrates self-disclosure and that it is okay to admit we are not perfect at valuing diversity. The story should also demonstrate that you are a champion of diversity as both a business issue and as a skill which will personally benefit you in the future.

TELL people about the session's purpose and agenda.

00:05 **Diversity Definitions and Terms**

REFER to the overhead, Diversity Defined (page 274).

ASK

• What stands out to you in this definition?

LISTEN for answers such as:

• Diversity is an asset, rather than a burden.

• Diversity includes everyone.

• Diversity is a mosaic, rather than a melting pot.

SAY in summary:

• We are defining diversity differently than you might expect. We
   see it as an asset to this organization, and as an issue that
   includes and benefits everyone.

REFER to the handout, Diversity Definitions and Terms (page 171).

ASK

• What questions do you have about the definitions?

SAY in summary:

• These definitions give us a common language for discussing diversity.

136

suggested actions

supporting material

Understanding the Icons

Major activities

The following icons mark major activities:

Activities that feature facilitator commentary. In these activities, you—as facilitator—present information that will be key to subsequent workshop activities.

Activities carried out in table groups. You assign participants to small groups to complete the activity at hand.

Activities to be completed on an individual basis.

Activities that revolve around group discussion. Such activities typically follow major exercises on which participants have worked individually or in groups. This icon is also used as a signal to listen for specific comments.

Supporting activities

The following icons mark supporting activities:

An overhead transparency is to be shown. The title of the overhead transparency is referenced in the text accompanying the icon.

An optional video that may be incorporated into the workshop.

A participant handout, part or all of a learning activity, or an assessment is to be handed out.

A question is to be asked. Wording for the question is provided, as are suggested answers when appropriate.

A flipchart is to be used. If the flipchart is one of the "prepared flipcharts" recommended for the workshop, its title will appear in the accompanying text.

Notes

Indicates a special note or suggested pre-work.

Indicates when to call time for timed exercises.

Marks the end of an exercise or section.

Using the Training Plans Effectively

One-day workshop

The one-day workshop incorporates most of the handouts, activities, overheads, and instruments contained in this sourcebook. For the most impact in your diversity training, it is recommended that you use the one-day format because it gives people the greatest opportunity to work through their thoughts and feelings about diversity through experiential self-discovery, and make a commitment to future actions which support diversity.

Half-day workshop

The half-day workshop has similar objectives to the one-day, but omits some of the experiential segments which require more time. It is a solid workshop designed to produce lasting results, but does not encompass the richness of experiential self-discovery that the one-day workshop includes. It also omits the segment on managing diversity found in the one-day workshop.

One-hour workshop

The one-hour workshops can be used in different ways, some as a prelude to or substitute for a full diversity workshop, some as add-ons. Two of them can be stand-alone, and two need to be used with one of the longer workshops. If you need several hours of workshop time but in shorter segments (60 to 90 minutes, for example) you can also tailor the one- or half-day workshops to meet your needs.

Group size

Because of the interactive nature of diversity workshops, as well as the need for self-disclosure and self-discovery, size must be limited to maintain a feeling of intimacy. Recommended group size is 12 to 18. A group with fewer than 12 does not yield a richness of interaction, while more than 18 can be unmanageable. With two co-facilitators, a size of 20 can be effective.

If possible, groups should be selected for a maximum of diversity within the group rather than a homogeneous composition. Training whole teams together can be very effective, so long as the manager doesn't dominate the group. In sessions with people from mixed departments, avoid placing managers with those who report directly to them because this can deter people from being honest.

Timing

The workshop guides contain suggested times for everything the trainer does. These are only guidelines, and in reality they rarely occur with exact precision. This is normal and to be expected. While the guidelines don't need to be followed rigidly, they give you a gauge for the overall progress of the session and indicate whether you need to shorten or omit an activity to make up for lost time.

Facilitation Format

Descriptions In the workshop guides, you will find information on the facilitation format of each segment or activity. Following is a description of each format, with suggested optimal uses.

Presentation This is when the trainer speaks briefly and concisely to reinforce important learning points or concepts from the pre-work. Try to limit the duration to five consecutive minutes or less, preferably with participants interjecting their own ideas or comments. Another option is to use questions to draw the information out of participants, rather than disseminating it yourself. Using vivid personal stories or organizational examples is an excellent way to enhance these segments.

Discussion During discussions, the trainer states an idea and then asks the group questions. It is sometimes necessary to rephrase or ask several different questions to generate responses. If people don't respond, allow silence. Humor can also break the ice, with statements like, "Is anybody out there?" Discussions are used to stimulate the group's thinking, initiate a dialogue, debrief a video, and encourage disagreement. Discussions also engage people with ideas more briefly than partner activities or group activities do.

Individual This is when people work individually on tasks which are usually either of a personal nature, or require that people collect their thoughts individually before a larger group activity.

Partners This is a quick, nonthreatening way to get people active and involved. It is also good for sensitive issues people might not discuss with a larger group. The trainer assigns partners quickly to speed the process. This is a good mode to loosen up a quiet group of individuals.

Group In the small-group mode, people give extended thought and share ideas with others to apply concepts to specific questions or situations. Because the small-group mode is more time consuming, it should be used only for important activities. Make sure directions are clear, and monitor groups to get a feel for their progress. Give time parameters up front, but be flexible if people need more time. Conclude when the majority of people are done even if a few are still working, otherwise people will begin to stray from the task.

Pre-workshop Communication and Marketing

Setting the appropriate tone for a diversity workshop through effective marketing and communications is crucial. Often, pre-workshop communication is overlooked or not used as fully as it could be for maximum effect.

Following are several steps you can take to heighten the impact of your diversity training. While all of these steps are not required, incorporating as many of them as possible increases the interest in and momentum of your effort.

Diversity communication and marketing includes:

- ☑ **Naming the workshop**

- ☑ **Kickoff announcements and memos**

- ☑ **Diversity celebrations**

- ☑ **Pre-work/manuals**

- ☑ **Email or Voice mail reminder**

- ☑ **Individual contact with participants before the session**

- ☑ **Officer kickoff and workshop participation**

Naming the Workshop

While it may seem like a minor point, the name of the workshop is important because it is how the effort will be referred to and remembered. It helps to have a group of people, representing all areas of the company, brainstorm a name. If this is not feasible, you can call a sampling of people individually to bounce ideas off them and get their feedback. Possible names include:

- Valuing Diversity

- Valuing and Managing Diversity

- Working Together Productively

- Working Together in a Team Environment

- Valuing Differences

- Valuing Diversity at _____ (Organization Name)

- Others?

Kickoff Announcements and Memos

A formal announcement from the president is a notable way to begin an effort of this magnitude. It catches people's attention and plants seeds that the organization's commitment to diversity is more than just lip service.

If possible, the memos should incorporate elements from the organizational assessment and strategy information which links diversity to your organization's business goals. Following are samples of kickoff and announcement memos. The kickoff announcement should be sent when the effort is started. The invitation memos can be sent with the pre-work, a few weeks prior to the workshop.

Sample Letters

**President's
kickoff letter**

Fellow Employee,

On _____, this organization will launch an effort which is of critical importance.

This effort is focused on bringing together all employees as a team of people who respect, trust, and appreciate each other as professionals. It's an effort which will help all of us to value each others' similarities as well as differences. *It will help us value diversity.*

Diversity is important to this organization for many reasons. It's important because we need to be innovative; we *need* a variety of ideas and perspectives to help us see business situations in new ways. Diversity is important because our customer base has become very diverse—and if we don't understand our customers, we'll miss opportunities and lag behind our competition. It's important because our employees are becoming more diverse, and we need to maintain our teamwork while at the same time encouraging a wide variety in people's backgrounds, viewpoints, and styles.

This organization has made a strong commitment to this effort. *Every single employee, including myself,* will participate in a workshop on diversity. In this workshop, we'll learn about the trends in society which make diversity a reality. We'll also learn ways to understand each other and work together more effectively.

To kick off the diversity effort, we will sponsor a series of events which will be both fun and educational. The first event, this Friday, will include complimentary lunch with a variety of ethnic foods and music, and casual day for all employees.

In these changing times, we need to pull together as a team to ensure our success. I know I can count on you to do that by sharing the company's belief in valuing *all* its employees.

Sincerely,

President

**President's
workshop
announcement**

Dear _____,

I would like to take a minute to personally invite you to our orga-nization's workshop on diversity.

You may be wondering, "Why are we spending time and effort on this during a year when we're working so hard to achieve our goals?" I'll tell you why. *People* and *teamwork* are what give us the ability to achieve our goals. As we've grown over the last few years, and as the workforce has changed, maintaining our team spirit has become more challenging. In addition, the consumers who buy our products—and keep us in business, I might add—have become very diverse, too.

I think we need to pay attention to valuing and managing diver-sity if we're going to stand out as the leader in our field.

Two weeks before the workshop, you will be sent some pre-work. I strongly encourage you to dedicate some quiet, quality time to completing it at least one week before the workshop you're scheduled to attend. Completing the reading and activities will take about 30 minutes, and is well worth your time.

Your scheduled session is listed on the following sheet. Please call _____ by _____ to either confirm your attendance, or schedule for another date. I know the workshop will be as informative and interesting for you as it was for me when I participated.

In these changing times, we need to pull together as a team to ensure our success. I know I can count on you to do that by shar-ing the company's belief in valuing *all* of our employees.

Sincerely,

President

**Generic participant
workshop invitation**

Hello!

Diversity is a critical issue in our organization's future success, because *people* and *teamwork* are what give us the ability to maintain our team spirit with a changing workforce. In addition, the customers who buy our products and services have become very diverse and we need to understand them to retain our competitive advantage.

To address these changes, this organization has committed to creating an environment in which we value diversity. Part of this is the diversity workshop program, which consists of the attached prework, as well as a workshop. Your manager has already participated in the management version of this program.

As you read in your letter from our president, you will need to dedicate some quiet, quality time to the workbook prior to attending the workshop. Completing the reading and activities will take about 30 minutes, and is crucial for your participation in the workshop. Be sure to complete the Diversity Statistics Quiz and Self-Assessment and bring them and your workbook to the session with you.

The workshop will last from _____ to _____ on the date listed on the following page. Your manager is aware that you will be attending, but please be sure to make him or her aware of the specific date. Dress for the day is casual and lunch will be provided. Please call _____ by _____ if you have any questions regarding the workshop or scheduling.

We look forward to working with you in creating an environment which values and celebrates diversity!

Training Manager

Generic letter to participant's manager

Hello!

Thank you for your active participation in this organization's diversity effort. Because of the enthusiasm and support of managers such as yourself, we are making excellent progress in establishing an environment which values diversity.

As you will remember from the diversity workshop, your position as a role model is critically important. Your staff will look to you to see how this effort is going to take shape in this organization.

In the next several months, the people who report to you will be scheduled to participate in the nonmanagement version of the workshop you attended. This program consists of pre-work and a workshop. The pre-work is shorter than what you completed and will take your staff members about 30 minutes to complete.

Now is a perfect opportunity for you to "walk the talk" of valuing diversity by actively encouraging your team members in their diversity education efforts. Your interest will make a big difference in helping people through the learning curve. You might want to consider including diversity as a topic at your next staff meeting, sending a voice mail message to team members in support of the effort, or using your creativity to think of other ways to be a role model.

As we move toward the year 2000, your role becomes even more important in helping make our organization a leader by creating an environment which understands and appreciates the diversity of our customers and employees. Much success in your efforts!

Training Manager

Diversity Celebrations

Diversity celebrations are a fun and educational way to spread the word of diversity and generate employee involvement and momentum.

One way to do this is to have volunteers create a "Diversity Celebration" day or days, in which various groups develop educational materials, entertainment, and food to share with the rest of the organization. Diversity groups and/or days can focus on any primary or secondary dimension, and might include:

- Gender groups (women's and/or men's)

- Ethnic groups (African-American, Hispanic, Asian, Native American, "Ellis Island Immigrants," etc.)

- Domestic situation groups (working moms, gays/lesbians, etc.)

- Company history groups (union people, specific divisions, professions, etc.)

It is important that the events are not positioned in such a way that the information presented reinforces stereotypes. The most positive way to position the celebrations is to have groups share educational information on the history of their groups, as well as contributions that their groups or prominent people from their groups have made to society or the workplace. Music, dance, and art created by the group can also be effective without reinforcing stereotypes.

Each group can be given a budget and guidelines with which to produce their event. Following are sample guidelines for diversity groups and how they might operate. Depending on budget, you could have a diversity celebration every month, bimonthly, etc. to maintain the momentum.

Diversity Events Committee Purpose and Guidelines

Purpose

Diversity events serve two purposes:

- To increase employees' value for diversity by providing a forum in which people can learn more about various groups.

- To help employees feel pride in their backgrounds by helping educate fellow employees about their elements of diversity.

The first priority of the events is education. The second priority is fun and entertainment. Fun and food can be useful to draw people in to an appreciation and educational experience of diversity.

Events are linked to organization goals

A diversity events committee will focus its educational efforts on the ways in which its group relates to achieving the organization's vision. Ideas might be:

- How have members of this group been positive role models?

- What positive contributions to society and business has this group made?

- What are common dilemmas or difficulties this group faces in the workplace?

- What are common misperceptions about this group which need to be overcome?

- How does having this element of diversity affect this group in the workplace?

- How can other groups interact with this group in ways which value their diversity?

Educational media include guest speakers, videos, posters, art work, festivities (dance, music), handouts, vendors, nonprofit organizations, and displays (clothing, crafts, literature).

Groups provide literature

Diversity committees will contribute updates and information to the diversity newsletter, and have a one-page handout of their mission, purpose, membership, and activities and how to join at their event.

Groups manage themselves responsibly

Diversity committees are responsible for all aspects of their event. This includes scheduling and promotion as well as easy-to-forget tasks such as room setup and cleanup. Committee members should be assigned to these tasks to ensure they are taken care of. Diversity chairpersons are responsible for staying within their group's budget.

Committees are inclusive

All committees will be open to participation by any employee, even if they do not have the background of the group. The more participation, the better, and everyone's ideas will be listened to. Decisions are to be made based on the collective creativity of the group.

Pre-work/Manual

The handouts in Chapter 6 contain information you can use "as is," to create pre-work for your workshop. Pre-work is important because it allows people to start thinking about diversity before going to the workshop. Because this is a topic that requires self-reflection, the advance "thinking time" makes the workshop more meaningful for people. As designed, the pre-work should take no more than 30 to 45 minutes to complete.

Each of the workshop guides chapters contains a checklist of the handouts/pre-work needed for that training design. To create a workbook, all you need to do is photocopy the materials, create a cover (a sample follows) and have it bound or put into a folder.

You need to customize the handout called Our Organization's Value for Diversity with your own specific initiatives and plans for supporting diversity, which reinforce why your organization is undertaking a diversity effort. An example of a customized sample of the handout follows.

The pre-work also needs to be accompanied by logistics information, telling people about the pre-work and how the workshop is structured. This could be the first page of the pre-work, or could be included in the cover memo. Following is a sample of logistics information.

Valuing and Managing Diversity

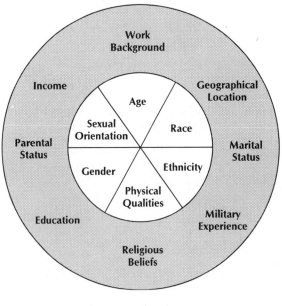

Participant Name
Company
Date

Sample cover sheet for pre-work workbook

Our Organization's Value for Diversity

This organization has launched a new and exciting effort to help us achieve our business goals now and in the years to come. In our desire to make the most of current trends in both the marketplace and the workforce, we have begun a process to create an environment which truly values diversity.

You may wonder why we are undertaking this effort, during a time of high market pressures, fierce competition, and the need to increase our efficiency. Many studies have demonstrated that companies which value diversity are consistently more innovative, more attuned to the marketplace and workforce, and have a more productive team environment. You will learn more about this when you participate in an upcoming diversity workshop.

After doing extensive research, we are convinced that this effort will have a positive bottom-line impact in helping us achieve our business goals. In our research, we first looked at the unique elements of our organization that prompted us to pay attention to the issue of diversity. The key ones for us were to:

- Adapt to population statistics of *Workforce 2000*
- Better understand our customers
- Compete for the best employees
- Foster innovation and well-rounded perspectives on decisions
- Support organizational goals
- Understand other organization's cultures during mergers
- Reduce legal or affirmative action problems
- Reduce conflict among diverse groups of employees
- Support our organization's values
- Do the right thing

Our organizational climate

Next, we did an organizational climate survey to determine where we are now in relation to where we want to be. We uncovered some strengths to build upon, as well as some obstacles to overcome.

Overwhelmingly, people feel that our company *cares about people*. One of the reasons why people like working here is that the company values *teamwork*. Our employees acknowledge the fact that it takes strong *interpersonal communication* skills to get ahead here. People are encouraged to *innovate*, and come up with new ideas; we like to be on the leading edge. And with the challenges our industry is facing, there are regular *opportunities* to become involved in new projects and learn.

All these attributes make our company a dynamic place to work, where people can gain satisfaction from *being part of a team* and collaborating with others, as well as making an individual contribu-

collaborating with others, as well as making an individual contribution. In fact, our president has been known to say that "it's our teamwork that gives us an edge." However, because of the changes in the workplace, as well as within our own company, *working together productively* is becoming increasingly challenging. The mergers we've experienced, the new divisional structure, new faces, changing job descriptions...all have made it more critical than ever that we maintain our team spirit. How do we do this when the "team" now consists of nearly 5,000 people, all from different backgrounds, different parts of the U.S. or the world, with different values, lifestyles, etc.? It's tempting to think that "my job would be so much easier if everyone were the same—or even better, if everyone were just like me!"

In particular, we found that people feel a significant gap between management and non-management, and we would like to take this opportunity to help bridge these differences and understand each other better. We also found some issues around the fact that women have entered jobs traditionally held by men in our company. Both of these issues will be discussed and addressed in this diversity effort.

Our organization culture of valuing people and communicating effectively gives us a head start. Because we're innovative, we want to be on the leading edge in preparing for the new marketplace and the new workforce. And because there is so much opportunity here, we'll probably experience diversity in both our customer base and our fellow employees.

Many of you participated in this study; thanks for your input. We have determined several ways to use these strengths and overcome these obstacles, which you will hear more about in the workshop.

Key infrastructures

We also assessed the key infrastructures which need to be in place to make this effort succeed. It is not enough for people to just be nicer to each other; the organization needs to update outmoded systems which may hinder the effort. As such, we examined:

- Recruiting
- Performance management
- Compensation
- Benefits
- Communication
- Events
- Training
- Education

In the workshop, you'll find out more about how we did in our assessment, as well as our plans for expanding and enhancing some of these infrastructures in the future.

Our organization is committed to creating an environment which truly values diversity, and we are prepared to "walk the talk" not only through workshops, but through the vehicles that really make this organization run.

We know you will find the diversity workshop in which you participate informative, engaging, and thought-provoking. If you have any questions, comments, or ideas on this effort prior to or after the session, please contact Mary Smith, Training Manager, at x4356.

Logistics Information

The *Valuing and Managing Diversity* workshop consists of the following six segments:

1. Introduction
2. What Is Diversity?
3. Analyzing Our Perceptions
4. Working Together Productively
5. Managing Diversity
6. Bringing It All Together

Program objectives

The overall objectives of the program are to:

- Ensure that participants understand our philosophy on diversity.

- Develop participants' appreciation of diversity as an asset.

- Help participants examine their own perceptions and behaviors regarding people who are different from themselves.

- Increase participants' skills in working productively with people who are different from themselves.

Valuing and Managing Diversity has two segments: pre-work and workshop.

Pre-work

The pre-work has been written in an informal, easy-to-read style with activities for you to fill out—so keep your pencil handy. It should take no more than 45 minutes to complete. It is *essential that you complete this pre-work* to participate in the workshop. The workbook contains activities that you will be required to share with others, so it is highly recommended that you arrive prepared. The self-assessments are for your use only, and can be very helpful in identifying areas that deserve your attention. It's critical that you *be honest with yourself.* Your ratings are confidential; you will share only as much or as little as you like with the group.

Workshop activities

The workshop will consist primarily of interactive activities based on the pre-work. *Please bring your pre-work with you.* There will be very little "lecture," so be prepared to participate, share your thoughts, and interact with fellow participants. In keeping with our company spirit, it will be fun!

The *Valuing and Managing Diversity* workshop will last all day, starting promptly at 8 a.m. Be sure people in your department know you will be unavailable. Breaks will be included for you to stretch or make rest stops, but phone calls will need to wait until the lunch break. Lunch will be provided. Attire is business casual. We look forward to seeing you there!

Email or Voice Mail Reminder

Email and voice mail provide an easy vehicle for reminding people about the session logistics and pre-work. You can send a reminder a few days before the session. An outline for the reminder might include:

- Time

- Location

- Attire for the day

- Trainer name

- Name of officer kicking off the session

- Food, lunch, telephone logistics

- Reminder to do pre-work

- Who to call for further information

- Looking forward to seeing them there

Individual Contact With Participants

If possible, it is helpful to informally make contact with each participant before the session. This is a good way to gauge people's feelings about the workshop, and to address any concerns or hesitations before the group convenes. It also adds a personal touch, and helps the facilitator to build rapport with participants.

If this is not possible, the trainer can at least greet people as they enter the room, shake hands, and introduce himself or herself.

Officer Kickoff and Workshop Participation

Having officers kickoff and/or participate in workshops is one of the most powerful tools a trainer can employ in demonstrating the organization's commitment to diversity.

It is recommended that any diversity effort include senior management as participants in the training themselves. This can be done with them as a separate group. Even better, they can participate one or two at a time along with the rest of the employees. Having senior managers in sessions with everyone else is powerful, and gives them a "reality check" of what's really going on in the organization. It also demonstrates true "walking the talk."

If they do participate with the rest of the employees, senior managers need to be coached beforehand on their role during the session. Regardless of their desire to be "just one of the group," everyone will look to them for reinforcement and role modeling. Officers do not have to pretend they are perfect at diversity; they only need to demonstrate a desire to learn and improve, and a verbal commitment to following through after the workshop. It is suggested that you talk with them privately beforehand to let them know how to maximize their participation for the greatest impact.

Once officers have participated in the workshop, they can act as kickoff speakers, lending their endorsement and support. Their talk does not need to be long; it is simply their presence that in many cases means the most. Again, they must be coached so their message is consistent with the workshop. Following is an outline to guide officers in preparing their kickoff speeches.

Senior Manager's Introduction/Kickoff Outline

Overview

Your presence in kicking off the workshop is a strong statement of our organization's commitment to the diversity effort. It is a signal to employees that you are prepared to actively "walk the talk" of diversity.

Your introduction only needs to be 2 to 3 minutes long. The primary message to communicate is that diversity is important to this organization, and you personally are committed to supporting it in word and action.

Outline

- Welcome
- Introduce yourself (name, position, length of service)
- Diversity is important to this organization's future
- Endorsement of the workshop—what you got out of it when you participated in it
- Your personal commitment to walking the talk
- Introduction/endorsement of trainer

Preparing Facilities, Equipment, and Supplies

Logistics preparation for diversity workshops includes site selection and setup, arranging for equipment, copying materials, obtaining overheads, preparing flipcharts, obtaining a class roster, setting up name tents and participant materials, and arranging the room. Each workshop guide contains a detailed checklist of all the materials you will need from this workbook. Following are samples of:

- Materials checklist
- Room setup diagrams
- Participant roster
- Name tents
- Workshop certificate

Both the name tents and certificates can be photocopied onto heavier, high-quality paper and used "as is." Or, if you want to customize them with your organization's logo, you can use the format as a guideline for creating your own graphics.

Materials Checklist

Equipment
- ☐ Four flipcharts
- ☐ Overhead projection screen
- ☐ VHS VCR and monitor

For each participant
- ☐ Name tents
- ☐ Notepads
- ☐ Pencils
- ☐ Markers (all identical)
- ☐ Handouts

Instructor materials
- ☐ Step-by-step training plan
- ☐ Prepared flipcharts
- ☐ Flipchart markers
- ☐ Overheads
- ☐ Overhead markers
- ☐ Masking tape
- ☐ Video, "A Class Divided" (optional, but recommended)
- ☐ Participant roster

Miscellaneous
- ☐ Ethnic foods for lunch, breaks
- ☐ Noisemakers, koosh balls, etc.
- ☐ Special items (from the trainer's guide)
- ☐ Diversity music tape
- ☐ Audiotape player
- ☐ Giveaway items (with The Platinum Rule on them)

Room Setup Diagrams

Fan-shaped

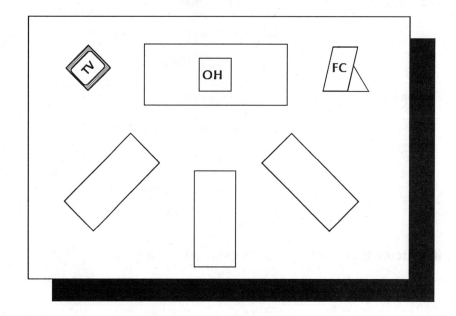

Round tables

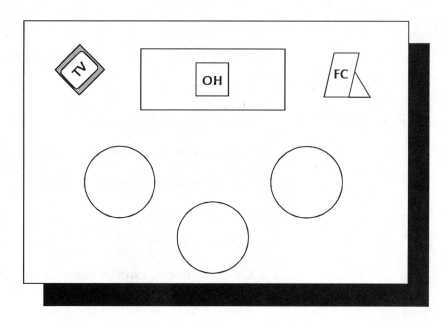

TV = Television or VCR
OH = Overhead
FC = Flipchart

Participant Roster

Trainer(s): _____

Date: _____   **Time:** _____

Location: _____

_____

	Participant Name	Extension	Department
1.	_____	_____	_____
2.	_____	_____	_____
3.	_____	_____	_____
4.	_____	_____	_____
5.	_____	_____	_____
6.	_____	_____	_____
7.	_____	_____	_____
8.	_____	_____	_____
9.	_____	_____	_____
10.	_____	_____	_____
11.	_____	_____	_____
12.	_____	_____	_____
13.	_____	_____	_____
14.	_____	_____	_____
15.	_____	_____	_____
16.	_____	_____	_____
17.	_____	_____	_____
18.	_____	_____	_____

Name Tent

Valuing and Managing
Diversity

Valuing and Managing
Diversity

Participant Name

Participant Name

Workshop Certificate

Certificate of Achievement

This certifies that, on

_____
(date)

_____
(name)

successfully completed the

Valuing and Managing Diversity

workshop

Congratulations!

_____
(Training Manager)

Chapter Three

A One-Day Diversity Workshop

This chapter of *The ASTD Trainer's Sourcebook*: *Diversity* contains the training plan for your one-day diversity workshop—ready to go "as is" or to be tailored to meet your needs.

CHAPTER OVERVIEW

This chapter is divided into six parts:

- Purpose of the workshop
- Workshop agenda
- Materials needed
- Suggested flipcharts
- Tailoring tips
- The step-by-step, one-day training plan

The one-day workshop is designed for all audiences. It also includes an optional 50-minute segment on the topic of managing diversity, which can be included if the participants are managers or omitted if they are nonmanagers.

Purpose of the Workshop

This workshop has six overall purposes. When participants have completed the session they will:

- Understand what valuing diversity is.
- Understand why valuing diversity is important for them as individuals.
- Understand why the organization is undertaking a diversity effort.
- Be able to analyze their own perceptions on diversity.
- Be able to behave in ways that value diversity.
- Be able to create a personal action plan for valuing diversity in the workplace.

Workshop Agenda

1. **Workshop Introduction**	Minutes 50	Start / Stop 8:00 / 8:50	Actual Start / Stop
Welcome			
Senior Manager Kickoff	5	8:00 / 8:05	_____ / _____
Trainer Personal Story	5	8:05 / 8:10	_____ / _____
Workshop Guidelines	5	8:10 / 8:15	_____ / _____
On the Outside (With Goals)	30	8:15 / 8:45	_____ / _____
Workshop Agenda Logistics	5	8:45 / 8:50	_____ / _____

2. **What Is Diversity?**	Minutes 1 hr. 20	Start / Stop 8:50 / 10:10	Actual Start / Stop
Diversity Definition and Terms	5	8:50 / 8:55	_____ / _____
Primary and Secondary Dimensions	5	8:55 / 9:00	_____ / _____
Diversity Statistics Quiz	20	9:00 / 9:20	_____ / _____
Workplace Trends	5	9:20 / 9:25	_____ / _____
Diversity History and Approaches	5	9:25 / 9:30	_____ / _____
Advantages of Diverse Groups	5	9:30 / 9:35	_____ / _____
Stepping Stones	30	9:35 / 10:05	_____ / _____
Our Organization's Plans, Commitment	5	10:05 / 10:10	_____ / _____
Break	15	10:10 / 10:25	_____ / _____

3. **Analyzing Our Perceptions**	Minutes 1 hr. 40	Start / Stop 10:25 / 12:05	Actual Start / Stop
How We Form Perceptions	5	10:25 / 10:30	_____ / _____
Stereotypes	25	10:30 / 10:55	_____ / _____
Prejudice or Excluding Others	30	10:55 / 11:25	_____ / _____
Valuing Diversity Self-Assessment	10	11:25 / 11:35	_____ / _____
Bests and Worsts	30	11:35 / 12:05	_____ / _____
Lunch	60	12:05 / 1:05	_____ / _____
Break (optional)	15	12:05 / 12:15	_____ / _____
Video, "A Class Divided" (optional)	40	12:15 / 12:55	_____ / _____

4. **Working Together Productively**	**Minutes** **1 hr. 45**	**Start / Stop** **1:05 / 2:50**	**Actual Start / Stop**
Behavior Basics	5	1:05 / 1:10	_____ / _____
Collusion	5	1:10 / 1:15	_____ / _____
The Platinum Rule	5	1:15 / 1:20	_____ / _____
Learning About Each Other	60	1:20 / 2:20	_____ / _____
Giving Feedback	30	2:20 / 2:50	_____ / _____
Break	15	2:50 / 3:05	_____ / _____

5. **Managing Diversity**	**Minutes** **50**	**Start / Stop** **3:05 / 3:55**	**Actual Start / Stop**
Managing Diversity Versus Traditional Management	15	3:05 / 3:20	_____ / _____
Key Factors for Managing Diversity	20	3:20 / 3:40	_____ / _____
Manager/Employee Interview Questions	10	3:40 / 3:50	_____ / _____
Managing Diversity Self-Assessment	5	3:50-3:55	_____ / _____

6. **Bringing It All Together**	**Minutes** **1 hr. 10**	**Start / Stop** **3:55 / 5:05**	**Actual Start / Stop**
Real-Life Case Studies or Derailment Case for Managers	20	3:55 / 4:15	_____ / _____
A Vision of Valuing Diversity	20	4:15 / 4:35	_____ / _____
Changes in Viewpoint on Diversity	5	4:35 / 4:40	_____ / _____
Learning Curve/Stages of Change	5	4:40 / 4:45	_____ / _____
Stereotypes Ceremony	5	4:45 / 4:50	_____ / _____
Valuing Diversity or Managing Diversity Action Plan	5	4:50 / 4:55	_____ / _____
Summary and Review of Goals	5	4:55 / 5:00	_____ / _____
Workshop Reactions	5	5:00 / 5:05	_____ / _____

Materials Needed

Following are checklists of materials recommended for the one-day diversity workshop. Except for the flipcharts, masters for the materials are found in the other chapters of this book. Flipcharts are illustrated in the next section. Unless otherwise noted:

- Make one handout and instrument per participant and send them as pre-work.

- Make one overhead transparency of each one needed.

- Prepare one of each flipchart needed.

Handouts / Pre-work

Send as pre-work:

☐ Our Organization's Value for Diversity, page 43 (to be customized for your organization)

☐ Diversity Definitions and Terms, page 171

☐ Workplace Trends and Statistics, page 174

☐ The History of Diversity, page 176

☐ Approaches to Diversity, page 178

☐ Advantages of Diverse Groups, page 180

☐ How We Form Perceptions, page 182

☐ Stereotyping, page 184

☐ Prejudice, page 185

☐ Behavior Basics, page 186

☐ Collusion, page 187

☐ The Platinum Rule, page 188

Additional pre-work if audience is management:

☐ Managing Diversity Versus Traditional Management, page 189

☐ How Managers Set a Tone for Diversity, page 190

☐ Diversity Employment Issues for Managers, page 193

☐ Team Guidelines and Communication for Managers, page 198

Instruments

Use before the workshop to customize for your organization:

☐ Organizational Climate Survey, page 245

☐ Organizational Reasons to Value Diversity, page 248

☐ Organization Diversity Strategies, page 250

Send as pre-work:

☐ Diversity Statistics Quiz, page 252

☐ Valuing Diversity Self-Assessment, page 259

☐ Managing Diversity Self-Assessment, page 263

☐ Manager / Employee Interview Questions, page 266

☐ Valuing or Managing Diversity Action, Plan (depending on audience), page 268 or 270

☐ Reaction Sheet, page 272

Activities

☐ Workshop Guidelines, page 202

☐ On the Outside (with Goals), page 204

☐ Primary / Secondary Dimensions, page 209

☐ Stepping Stones, page 211

☐ Stereotypes, page 212

☐ Bests and Worsts, page 219

☐ Learning About Each Other, page 220

☐ Excluding Others, page 222 (needed if not using the Prejudice segment and video: "A Class Divided")

☐ Giving Feedback, page 224

☐ Real-Life Case Studies or Derailment Case Study for Managers (depending on audience), page 237 or 239

☐ A Vision of Valuing Diversity, page 241

Overheads

☐ Diversity Defined, page 274

☐ Primary and Secondary Dimensions, page 275

☐ Diversity Statistics Quiz Answers, page 276

☐ Workplace Trends, page 277

☐ Approaches to Diversity, page 278

☐ Perceptions and Stereotypes, page 279

☐ Collusion Defined, page 280

☐ The Platinum Rule, page 281

☐ Changes in Viewpoint on Diversity, page 283

☐ Learning Curve, page 284

☐ Stages of Change, page 286

Flipcharts

☐ Workshop Guidelines, page 60

☐ Introductions, page 60

☐ Goals, page 61

☐ "One Word," page 61

☐ Workshop Agenda, page 61

☐ Stepping Stones, page 61

☐ Our Organization's Plans, page 62

☐ Stereotypes, page 62

☐ Bests and Worsts, page 62

☐ Learning About Each Other, page 62

☐ Giving Feedback Guidelines, page 63

☐ Key Factors for Managing Diversity, page 63

☐ A Vision of Valuing Diversity, page 63

Special Materials

☐ Welcome

- Senior Manager Kickoff Outline, page 47 (to be given before the session)

- Workshop Guidelines

- Fun items: noise makers, etc.

☐ Stepping Stones

- Small stones or Play-Doh (8 per participant)

☐ Real-Life Goals

- Feedback questionnaires, page 217

- Feedback summary envelopes (sent prior to the workshop)

☐ Prejudice

- Video: "A Class Divided" (optional, but recommended; see ordering information in Appendix)

☐ Key Factors for Managing Diversity

- 3-foot x 5-foot butcher paper

- Repositionable spray adhesive

- 8 1/2-inch x 5 1/2-inch colored paper

Suggested Flipcharts

Following are visual representations of the flipcharts listed on the previous page. Details of the timing and use for each can be found in the activity guides as well as in the step-by-step training plan which follows. Items which should be written on the flipchart *before* the session are represented below in **bold type**. Examples of items you will write in *during* the session are in *italics*. Notes for you regarding the flipchart are written in plain type or in parentheses. The sequence goes left to right, then down the page.

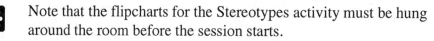

Remember to watch for the flipchart icon in the training plans.

Note that the flipcharts for the Stereotypes activity must be hung around the room before the session starts.

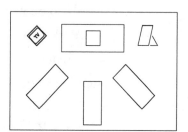

Make sure the flipchart can be readily seen from all seating locations in the training room.

Workshop Guidelines

- *Nothing we say leaves the room*
- *No personal attacks*
- *Don't interrupt people*
- *Everyone participates*
- *Be on time*

Introductions

- Name
- Department
- Length of Service
- "On the Outside"— story/one word
- Goal, Hope or Concern

Goals

- *Learn more about what bothers people*
- *Analyze my own biases*
- *Learn more about the company's plans*
- *Find ways to communicate better*
- *Have fun!*

"One Word"

- *Isolated*
- *Targeted*
- *Lonely*
- *Angry*
- *Demotivated*

Workshop Agenda

- What Is Diversity?
- Break
- Analyzing Our Perceptions
- Lunch
- Working Together Productively
- Break
- Managing Diversity
- Bringing It All Together (end at 5:05 p.m.)

Stepping Stones

What series of six to eight stepping stones has led this organization to the diversity environment it has today?

Our Organization's Plans

(Summary of plans, based on Our Organization handout and instrument results)

Society's Stereotypes of Accountants

(You will need ten flipcharts, each with a different element of diversity. Examples may include: Asians, Working Mothers, People with Military Background, Gays/Lesbians, People over 50, Catholics, Single People, MBAs, New Yorkers.)

*Do Not Use

* See note on next page.

"Bests"

- *Calling people on it when they tell an inappropriate joke*
- *Standing up for someone in a meeting*
- *Asking me how I want to be treated*

(You will also create a blank chart with "Worsts" at the top on which to write people's ideas.)

Learning About Each Other

- **What problems do you experience in the workplace in relation to the other group?**
- **What can the other group do differently to improve the situation?**
- **What is your group willing to do to help them?**

Giving Feedback Guidelines

- *No personal attacks*
- *Don't assume the worst*
- *Let the person save face*
- *Thank people when they give you feedback*

Key Factors for Managing Diversity

What managerial behaviors will create an environment and infrastructure that values diversity?

A Vision of Valuing Diversity

- **Brainstorm your vision of what this organization would be like if we truly valued diversity.**
- **Create a graphic representation of your vision.**
- **List two or three concrete actions that you—as an individual—can take to make the vision a reality.**

 The examples shown on "Society's Stereotypes of Accountants" are for illustrative purposes only. We suggest that you develop your own list of examples, and write (for legal reasons) "Do Not Use" at the bottom of each of the ten flipcharts used in the exercise.

Tailoring Tips

The one-day workshop can be tailored in a variety of ways. The most basic level of tailoring is to include your own personal anecdotes and modify the language to fit your own personal style.

Another type of tailoring is the use or non-use of pre-work. If you decide not to send pre-work, you will either need to have people read the handouts in the session, or you will need to do longer presentations on these topics. These segments will then take longer and you will need to eliminate some of the more experiential activities. It is *highly* recommended that you send pre-work instead, but both options are possible within the one-day format.

The workshop can also be tailored in the following ways:

- Add examples from your environment.

- Substitute other introduction/icebreaker activities.

- Substitute other experiential activities.

- Eliminate the management segment for a non-management audience (or to shorten to a three-fourth day workshop).

- Split it into shorter segments.

Adding examples from your experience can greatly enhance and "bring home" important points. To do this, reflect on your own experiences and ask others for examples which demonstrate particular points.

If you wish to substitute other icebreakers for the one suggested, you will find two others in the beginning of Chapter 7, Learning Activities. These are My Dimensions of Diversity on page 206 and What's My Line? on page 208. They are about the same length, so the workshop would not need to be modified in any other way.

If you wish to substitute other activities, you will find several which have not been used in the one-day workshop. These are described in detail, both in Chapter 7, Learning Activities, and in Chapter 5, Four One-Hour Diversity Workshops.

The Prejudice segment, which contains use of the video "A Class Divided," is highly recommended but not required. (See Appendix for ordering information.) If you choose not to purchase and use the video, you can substitute the activity, Excluding Others (page 222) or another activity of your choice.

You can also tailor (and shorten) this workshop by removing the segment on Managing Diversity. If you have a session in which all participants are nonmanagers, you may not need these activities. This also shortens the workshop by 50 minutes.

If you would like to do eight hours of training, but need to do it in shorter segments, you can split the design into segments that range in length from 45 minutes to 1 hour and 50 minutes. If you wish to do this, begin each session with a 5-minute review of the previous session, and end each session with a 5-minute preview of the upcoming session. This ensures continuity between the sessions.

Please note that the timing for the workshop as designed is very tight. If you prefer a more relaxed pace, or find yourself with a talkative group, you may want to omit an activity to allow for a time cushion.

Training Plan

Workshop Introduction

Overview

The purpose of this segment is to establish the importance of diversity to the organization, and to set a tone of openness, personal sharing, and self-directed learning for the session. You do this by being open yourself, sharing personal experiences, and building rapport with the group through interaction and humor.

Objectives

Upon completion of this segment, participants will be able to:

- Understand senior management's commitment to diversity.

- View the trainer as a role model of self-disclosure and continuous learning (rather than an "expert"), and as a diversity champion.

- Have a set of guidelines for the group in creating an environment of openness and giving each other feedback.

- Feel a sense of control and self-direction for their own learning by establishing their own goals and group norms.

- Empathize with people who are in the minority.

- Know something about all the other participants.

- Be warmed up, with everyone having shared in pairs and with the large group.

- Understand the logistics and agenda for the session.

Workshop Agenda

1. Workshop Introduction	Minutes 50	Start / Stop 8:00 / 8:50	Actual Start / Stop
Welcome			
Senior Manager Kickoff	5	8:00 / 8:05	_____ / _____
Trainer Personal Story	5	8:05 / 8:10	_____ / _____
Workshop Guidelines	5	8:10 / 8:15	_____ / _____
On the Outside (With Goals)	30	8:15 / 8:45	_____ / _____
Workshop Agenda Logistics	5	8:45 / 8:50	_____ / _____

1. Workshop Introduction (8:00 to 8:50)

00:05   **Senior Manager Kickoff**

 SAY that the session is starting, and move to the side of the room.

 DEMONSTRATE attention to the speaker and show nonverbal support (nodding, etc.) when important statements are made.

00:05   **Trainer Personal Story**

 TELL a personal story of your own learning about diversity, which demonstrates self-disclosure and that it is okay to admit we are not perfect at valuing diversity. The story should also demonstrate that you are a champion of diversity as both a business issue and as a skill which will personally benefit you in the future.

00:05   **Workshop Guidelines**

 SAY

- My role is not to be the "authority" in this workshop, but to be a guide to important information and ideas, and to facilitate our self-discovery.

- While valuing diversity is a personal decision people must make on their own, this organization also expects us to exhibit positive diversity behaviors which are consistent with the way we want to interact and do business.

- This workshop is a "laboratory" for people to test out their own ideas in relation to their peers, and that means we need to feel comfortable being open and sharing. You will get out of this session what you put in by participating.

- Disagreement is okay, and even encouraged—so long as it is done respectfully.

? *ASK*

- What do you need in order to feel comfortable opening up and disclosing today?

 SAY as an example:

- Sometimes groups want a guideline like, "Nothing we say leaves the room."

ASK

- What do you think of that one?

- If someone disagrees with you, how do you want them to express their disagreement?

LISTEN for answers that meet these criteria.

- Everyone agrees the guideline should be included.

They are observable behaviors.

CHART responses on the flipchart, Workshop Guidelines (page 60).

SAY in summary:

- This is *your* list, and *you* as a group will monitor and enforce it.

- I have brought fun tools for each table (noisemakers, koosh balls, etc.), which you can use to let each other know if there has been a violation. This gives us a lighthearted way to practice being open with feedback, and also makes it okay to have fun today.

00:30   **On the Outside (With Goals)**

SAY

- Now, we're going to do introductions, first with a partner, then for the entire group. This exercise will also help us better empathize with others who are "on the outside"—for example, someone who has an unpopular idea in a meeting, or the new person in the department.

REFER people to the flipchart, Introductions (page 60).

DEMONSTRATE by introducing yourself according to the points on the flipchart. Include both your full story *and* your "one word."

ASK participants to introduce themselves to their partners using both their full stories and their "one word."

MONITOR the group for 5 to 10 minutes while they work in pairs.

ASK for volunteers to introduce themselves and to share their "one word."

CHART participants' goals on one flipchart, and their "one word" on another. Post them for the duration of the session.

ASK, regarding the "one word" statements:

- How would someone who was feeling these things behave at work? How would this feeling affect someone's productivity?

- What impact would it have on a team if a member felt this way?

LISTEN for these types of answers.

- People wouldn't be very productive.

- This wouldn't create a positive work environment.

SAY in summary:

- Remembering how it feels to be on the outside can help us empathize with others.

- Think of the increased productivity and improved work environment we'd have by eliminating these feelings.

- Regarding our goals, we will (*or will not, as appropriate*) address these, and will review them at the end of the day.

00:05   **Workshop Agenda / Logistics**

REFER people to the flipchart, Workshop Agenda (page 61).

SAY

- Here is our agenda for the day. First, we'll come to a common understanding of how we define diversity, and why it's important. Then, we'll have a chance to analyze our own perceptions. After that, we'll look at ways to work together more productively. Next, we'll talk about how to manage diversity. Then, we'll do some activities which bring all these ideas together.

- We'll end with your action plan for valuing diversity. What's important isn't this workshop; it's what you do afterward that counts.

TELL people about the day's logistics, such as break times, ending time, food provided, restrooms, telephones, etc.

What Is Diversity?

Overview   The purpose of this segment is to help people understand what diversity is, and why it is important to the organization as well as to them as individuals. Because this segment provides the most information, you need to know your facts and figures. It also provides an early opportunity for people to voice concerns or questions about the topic. Participants may challenge you, and you should encourage this because it is better to have an open discussion than for people to "tune out" or let their questions go unaddressed.

A highlight of the segment is the Diversity Statistics Quiz, after which people often realize how out of touch they are with what's going on in society. The uncomfortable feelings then transition into "here's what we're doing about it," with your organization's diversity strategies. It is important to emphasize the organization's commitment in both word and action.

Objectives

Upon completion of this segment, participants will be able to:

- Use a common language in discussing diversity.

- Understand that diversity extends beyond the obvious characteristics of race and gender to include and liberate everyone.

- Test and expand their understanding of workplace demographic trends.

- Understand the history of diversity and approaches taken to address it.

- Understand that diversity is an asset rather than a burden to be tolerated.

- Analyze the organization's evolution in terms of diversity.

- Understand the organization's philosophy and plans on diversity.

Workshop Agenda

2. **What Is Diversity?**	Minutes 1 hr. 20	Start / Stop 8:50 / 10:10	Actual Start / Stop
Diversity Definition and Terms	5	8:50 / 8:55	_____ / _____
Primary and Secondary Dimensions	5	8:55 / 9:00	_____ / _____
Diversity Statistics Quiz	20	9:00 / 9:20	_____ / _____
Workplace Trends	5	9:20 / 9:25	_____ / _____
Diversity History and Approaches	5	9:25 / 9:30	_____ / _____
Advantages of Diverse Groups	5	9:30 / 9:35	_____ / _____
Stepping Stones	30	9:35 / 10:05	_____ / _____
Our Organization's Plans, Commitment	5	10:05 / 10:10	_____ / _____
Break	15	10:10 / 10:25	_____ / _____

2. What Is Diversity? (8:50 to 10:10)

00:05   **Diversity Definitions and Terms**

 REFER to the overhead, Diversity Defined (page 274)

 ASK

- What stands out to you in this definition?

 LISTEN for answers such as:
- Diversity is an asset, rather than a burden.
- Diversity includes everyone.
- Diversity is a mosaic, rather than a melting pot.

 SAY in summary:
- We are defining diversity differently than you might expect. We see it as an asset to this organization, and an issue that includes and benefits everyone.

 REFER to the handout, Diversity Definitions and Terms (page 171).

 ASK

- What questions do you have about the definitions?

 SAY in summary:
- These definitions give us a common language for discussing diversity. We will go over them in sections throughout the day.

00:05   **Primary and Secondary Dimensions**

 REFER people to the overhead and handout, Primary and Secondary Dimensions (pages 275 and 173, respectively).

 SAY

- In the 1991 book *Workforce America!*, authors Loden and Rosener define diversity in terms of two dimensions: primary and secondary.

- Primary dimensions are those that we are born with. People are usually the most sensitive about these dimensions because others can tell these things about us (with the exception of sexual preference) just by looking at us. So if someone has a preconceived idea about a certain dimension, they can project that onto someone before the person even opens his or her mouth.

- Secondary dimensions are those we have some control over, and they can change throughout our lives. People also have a choice of whether they want to disclose this information or not. So people usually aren't as sensitive about these dimensions, even though these may have as big an impact on who we are as the primary dimensions do.

? *ASK*

- What additional dimensions contribute to who we are as people, but aren't listed on the chart? What would you add?

👀 *LISTEN* for answers such as:

- Family upbringing, political affiliation, lifestyle, hobbies, etc.

- Personality type as a dimension can be reinforced by saying:

- How many people are familiar with the Myers-Briggs Type Inventory? It's an instrument which indicates our preference for one of 16 types. If you administered it to a group of 30-year-old white men and a group of 60-year-old Chinese women, both groups would split into the 16 types. You would find that a white man and a Chinese woman who had the same personality type actually *think* more like each other than the people who share demographic similarities.

📄 *WRITE* additions on the overhead around the outside of the diagram.

? *ASK*

- Who do you think the term "diversity" is referring to?

- Are we all equally "diverse," or are some of us more "diverse" than others?

📊 *SAY* in summary:

- Diversity extends far beyond the obvious dimensions of race and gender. People are similar and different on an infinite number of dimensions. By viewing the idea of "valuing diversity" as something that is equally relevant to all of us, it becomes inclusive as well as liberating for everyone.

00:20   **Diversity Statistics Quiz**

📄 *REFER* people to the instrument, and overhead (with answers), Diversity Statistics Quiz (pages 252 and 276, respectively).

📊 *TELL* people to calculate the number they answered incorrectly.

MONITOR people as they check their answers.

 ASK

- How did you do? Did you know as much about your environment as you thought you did?

- Are there any comments or questions on any of these statistics?

- How will these trends change the products and services we offer?

- How will the workplace be different because of these trends?

 LISTEN for answers such as:

- I didn't score as well as I thought I would. (*This is common.*)

- The workplace will be very different than in the past.

 SAY in review of the quiz and summary:

- In question number one, we can see that the workplace was created in ways which reflected the needs of the people who were originally in it. This is natural, and no one is "to blame." The problem is that the workplace has become outdated for the people who are in it *now*. (*Also see the answer sheet for other items to highlight.*)

- It is normal for people to score poorly on this quiz. It's just a demonstration that things have changed without us noticing. We need to embrace this new reality, and find ways of addressing diversity as an advantage which can enrich our workplaces and help us understand our customers better.

00:05   **Workplace Trends**

 REFER people to the handout and overhead, Workplace Trends and Statistics (pages 174 and 277, respectively).

 TELL people about the trends as indicated in the handout.

00:05   **Diversity History and Approaches**

 REFER people to the handouts, History of Diversity and Approaches to Diversity (pages 176 and 178, respectively), and the overhead, Approaches to Diversity (page 278).

ASK

- What happened during the "Golden Rule" period?

- What did you read about the "Right the Wrongs" approach?

- Why would we now want to "Value All Differences?"

LISTEN for answers such as:

- The "Golden Rule" approach had good intentions, but didn't allow for people to be different from the dominant culture.

- "Right the Wrongs" was a step in the right direction, but created an "us versus them" mentality and split people apart.

SAY in summary:

- We have evolved as a society to the point where we now are able to see diversity as an asset, rather than a process of quota-filling. Valuing diversity is the approach we are taking in this organization.

00:05   **Advantages of Diverse Groups**

REFER people to the handout, Advantages of Diverse Groups (page 180).

TELL people about the research highlighted in the handout.

00:30   **Stepping Stones**

TELL people they are going to do an activity identifying the six to eight key stepping stones that have led the organization to the diversity environment it has today. They will have 5 minutes to work individually. Then each person will have 3 to 4 minutes (20 minutes total) to describe their stepping stones. As people place their stones on the table, they will describe their observations about the stones and how the stones affected them.

REFER people to the flipchart, Stepping Stones (page 61), with the question, and the stones on their tables.

ASK

- What series of six to eight stepping stones has led this organization to the diversity environment it has today?

MONITOR people as they work through the activity.

ASK

- What was more significant: people or events?

- How would your view of these events be different, if the time frame was five years prior to now or five years from now?

LISTEN for answers such as:

- Both people and events were important.

- Our perspective changes over time.

SAY in summary:

- Everyone has their own perception of the organization, and all the perceptions are accurate, depending on whose eyes we see through.

- Reflecting on our organization can help us to understand the way things are today, as well as help us to determine key actions to create positive change in the future.

00:05   **Our Organization's Plans and Commitment**

REFER people to the handout, Our Organization's Value for Diversity (page 169) and the flipchart, Our Organization's Plans (page 62).

TELL people about your organization's commitment and plans, as highlighted in the handout.

ASK

- What do you think this organization will have to do to make this effort succeed?

- What questions do you have about our organization's commitment before we move on to analyzing our perceptions?

SAY in summary:

- This organization has chosen to view diversity as a bottom-line issue which is an asset to our business and includes everyone. As you can see, we are truly committed to creating an environment which values diversity.

00:15   **Break**

(Hang up flipcharts around the room in preparation for the Stereotypes activity.)

Analyzing Our Perceptions

Overview

The purpose of this segment is to help people understand how we form our perceptions, and to help them to analyze their own. This is a very important segment, in which trainers often see "light bulbs going off" in participants' minds.

The segment builds, starting with the idea the we all stereotype people and screen out contradictory facts. Then, people list stereotypes. The trainer needs to ask good questions so people discover on their own that they may be projecting inaccurate perceptions onto others; telling them is not nearly as effective. (The Stereotypes activity requires skilled facilitation, so you should review the full instructions on page 212 in Chapter 7.)

Use of the video, "A Class Divided," is highly recommended but not required. You can substitute the Excluding Others activity on page 222 if desired, or substitute another activity of your choice. (See the activity description for complete instructor information). If the video is used, during this segment people sometimes laugh (it is funny at times), or the room becomes quiet as people feel its impact. Usually, people see the dramatic impact of stereotyping and that it is often made up in our minds. This can be a turning point for people's self-realization and commitment to valuing diversity. Next, people assess their own skills and developmental areas. The segment ends with some high-energy brainstorming for a transition to the next section. Optional lunch activities provide for informal discussion and reflection on the day so far.

Objectives

Upon completion of this segment, participants will be able to:

- Understand how perceptions are formed and can turn into stereotypes.

- Discover how we form our perceptions.

- Identify common stereotypes and realize their negative impact.

- Assess their own skill level in valuing diversity.

- Identify best and worst examples of valuing diversity.

 The following video is optional, but recommended for this segment:

- "*A Class Divided*" (purchase $200, no rental available) VideoLearning Resource Group, 1-800-225-3959.

    (The first 20 minutes is used for the Prejudice activity, and as an option, the rest may be viewed at lunch.)

Workshop Agenda

3. Analyzing Our Perceptions	Minutes 1 hr. 40	Start / Stop 10:25 / 12:05	Actual Start / Stop
How We Form Perceptions	5	10:25 / 10:30	_____ / _____
Stereotypes	25	10:30 / 10:55	_____ / _____
Prejudice or Excluding Others	30	10:55 / 11:25	_____ / _____
Valuing Diversity Self-Assessment	10	11:25 / 11:35	_____ / _____
Bests and Worsts	30	11:35 / 12:05	_____ / _____
Lunch	60	12:05 / 1:05	_____ / _____
Break (optional)	15	12:05 / 12:15	_____ / _____
Video, "A Class Divided" (optional)	40	12:15 / 12:55	_____ / _____

3. Analyzing Our Perceptions (10:25 to 12:05)

00:05   **How We Form Perceptions**

REFER to the handout, How We Form Perceptions (page 182) and the overhead, Perceptions and Stereotypes (page 279).

TELL people about perceptions as described in the handout.

00:25   **Stereotypes**

REFER to the handout, Stereotyping (page 184).

SAY

- Stereotypes are a necessary part of the way our brains function. We have so much data coming at us, that our brains only actually pay attention to a small percentage of it. The rest is sorted by category so we don't have to think about it. Stereotypes become negative when we filter out evidence which contradicts our preconceived ideas.

- Now we're going to do an activity which helps us identify common stereotypes, based on a variety of the primary and secondary dimensions.

- Take a marker from your table. As quickly as you can, go around the room and write a stereotype that you are familiar with on each flipchart. The only rule is that you can't repeat one that is already listed. You will have 5 to 10 minutes to do this.

MONITOR people as they complete the activity.

 TELL people to take their seats and read the charts.

 ASK

- How did you feel writing the stereotypes down? Why?

- How do you feel, seeing all these stereotypes?

- What percentage are negative? Why are so many negative?

- Is anyone exempt from being stereotyped?

- How does it feel to know people may be stereotyping *you* in these ways?

- What impact does it have on a person, if we perceive that person according to what is on these flipcharts?

- Does anyone know of a person (other than yourself) who doesn't fit one of these stereotypes? When we do, is our tendency to change our stereotype, or to say "they're the exception?" (e.g., "He's not your typical New Yorker.")

- Do you think these stereotypes ever creep into this organization? What would happen if they did?

 LISTEN for answers such as:

- We focus on the negative, rather than the positive in people.

- Stereotypes apply to everyone, and everyone is hurt by them.

- Maybe we see what we're looking for, instead of what's really there.

- If someone contradicts the stereotype, we usually think they're the exception rather than change our stereotype.

- Seeing these things in people is a waste of energy, and hurts our productivity.

 SAY in summary:

- It took the group only about 5 minutes to come up with nearly X number (100, etc.) of stereotypes. If we had an hour, we could come up with thousands. Stereotypes are prevalent in our society, and we need to heighten our awareness of them to keep them from influencing our perceptions of others and to keep them from distorting our view of people as they really are.

00:30   **Prejudice (optional)**

SAY

- Often, people wonder where stereotypes come from. We're going to watch a video called "*A Class Divided.*" It's a PBS documentary, originally filmed in 1968, in which a teacher creates a microcosm of society in a third-grade classroom in an all-white, all-Christian farming community in Iowa. Although her focus is on racial issues, what you're about to see applies to all kinds of diversity issues. I think you'll find it pretty dramatic. It's about 20 minutes long.

PLAY the video, "A Class Divided," starting with "Good evening. Tonight on Frontline . . ." and ending with the children hugging after they take off their collars (before the teacher is interviewed).

ASK

- What are your reactions to this?

- Where did the stereotypes come from? How did the teacher create them?

- In applying this to society, or our organization, who or what fills the role of the teacher?

- Why do you think the "up" kids were so mean to their friends? Do we do this as adults?

- Why did the children's test scores go down? How does this happen in the workplace?

- Why did the children buy into the idea that they were in the "down" group, even on the second day when they knew it wasn't real? Do we do this to ourselves as adults?

- How do situations like the one in "A Class Divided" happen in the workplace?

LISTEN for answers such as:

- The teacher created the stereotypes by picking random examples, and then applying them broadly to the whole group.

- Authority figures such as leaders, or the media, have the same influence as the teacher.

- The kids were mean because they knew they could get away with it—it's a power game, just like that of adults.

See also the "Excluding Others" Learning Activity, page 222.

- The children's scores went down, just like a self-fulfilling prophecy. This also happens when people at work expect the worst from us, or when we buy into others' stereotypes of us.

- This happens all the time, with "in groups" and "out groups" at work, or with people whose characteristics or ideas are different from the dominant group.

SAY in summary:

- This video shows what happens when we allow prejudice and bias into any group, including the workplace. As an organization, we can't afford such an extreme waste of energy and productivity. Valuing diversity can help us to overcome this.

00:10   **Valuing Diversity Self-Assessment**

SAY

- Now we'll have a chance to see where we are in our own ability to value diversity.

REFER to the instrument, Valuing Diversity Self-Assessment (page 259).

TELL people this is for their own use only, and ask them to review their scores and the categories.

ASK

- What do each of the scoring categories mean to you?

- In which category do you think the organization would like everyone to score?

- How can you use this information in your efforts to better value diversity?

LISTEN for answers such as:

- "Naive" seems like it could be in any score range, because the person is unaware of his or her behavior.

- The organization would probably like us to be change agents.

- This gives me ideas of things I can do to show that I value diversity.

SAY in summary:

- While most people fall in the Traditional or Neutral categories, the organization is doing this diversity training to encourage more people to become Change Agents.

• You may want to create a diversity goal for yourself based on any items for which you scored yourself lower than you would like, and include it in your action plan at the end of the session.

00:30   **Bests and Worsts**

 SAY

• To start thinking about diversity behaviors, let's do a brainstorming activity. Call out your answers to these questions as quickly as you can think of them.

REFER to the flipcharts, Bests and Worsts (page 62).

• Chart participants' responses quickly on the appropriate flipchart.

TELL people to work in their small groups for 10 minutes to do the following:
• Create five "Do's" based on the "Bests" list.
• Create five "Don'ts" based on the "Worsts" list.

LISTEN as people report back to the large group with their summaries.

SAY in summary:

• Often, valuing diversity is a matter of common sense and it is easy to see practices which value diversity and those which do not.
• The key is being able to consistently *act* on this common sense.
• After lunch, we'll look at additional ways we can work together productively to create an environment which values diversity. This will give you some additional ideas on how to build on your strengths, develop your skills, and create diversity goals for your action plan.

ASK people if they would like to watch the rest of the video, "A Class Divided," during lunch. If they would, agree on the time you will begin to play it. (The remaining segment is about 40 minutes long.)

TELL people about lunch logistics, such as food, time to return, telephones, etc.

12:05 / 1:05   **Lunch**

Working Together Productively

Overview

The purpose of this segment is to help people learn new behaviors to create an environment that values diversity. The activities, Behavior Basics and Collusion, set the stage with a discussion of how and why diversity violations occur. We then move to the cornerstone of this segment: The Platinum Rule and how to use it. The activity, Learning About Each Other, is a vivid demonstration of this principle in practice, and usually has a strong impact on participants. If done well, the group will discover that it is not as hard as they thought to talk about difficult issues, and that they now have an easy format for doing so. They also usually learn something useful about the other group. It is important for you to encourage the groups to carry on a dialogue among themselves, rather than having them present information to you. The activity, Giving Feedback, provides solid practice for people in addressing diversity violations in a productive manner.

Objectives

Upon completion of this segment, participants will be able to:

- State the minimum legal requirements for diversity behavior.

- Recognize collusion, and how to avoid it.

- Describe the benefits of using The Platinum Rule.

- Communicate about difficult or taboo issues with others in an open way that values the other person or group.

- Address conflict and give negative feedback in a way that maintains value for the other person.

Workshop Agenda

4. Working Together Productively	Minutes 1 hr. 45	Start / Stop 1:00 / 2:45	Actual Start / Stop
Behavior Basics	5	1:05 / 1:10	_____ / _____
Collusion	5	1:10 / 1:15	_____ / _____
The Platinum Rule	5	1:15 / 1:20	_____ / _____
Learning About Each Other	60	1:20 / 2:20	_____ / _____
Giving Feedback	30	2:20 / 2:50	_____ / _____
Break	15	2:50 / 3:05	_____ / _____

4. Working Together Productively (1:05 to 2:50)

00:05   **Behavior Basics**

 REFER to the handout, Behavior Basics (page 186).

 TELL people about "behavior basics" as described in the handout.

 ASK

- How might examples like the ones listed on your handout be interpreted as creating a biased or harassing environment?

- What other words, expressions, phrases, or behaviors have you heard which you or others might find inappropriate or offensive?

 LISTEN for answers such as:

- These behaviors reinforce stereotypes and could be seen as devaluing people.

- In using The Platinum Rule, we find out whether these things bother someone or not, rather than assuming.

- Other inappropriate words might include the use of "guys" when referring to a group of people.

- Other inappropriate behaviors might include talking about sports or women's issues in a way which excludes another group.

 SAY in summary:

- These guidelines are the bare minimum in creating an environment which values diversity.

- The bottom line is this: Does it add value to workplace productivity? If it doesn't, and could potentially cause a problem, why do it?

00:05   **Collusion**

 REFER to the handout and overhead, Collusion (pages 187 and 280, respectively).

 ASK

- What kind of collusion do you think is most common?

- Why would people remain silent?

LISTEN for answers such as:

- People are afraid of being the next target.

- People don't want to risk their careers or their acceptance by the group.

 SAY in summary:

- Silence may seem harmless, but can reinforce stereotyping and a lack of value for diversity.

- An extreme example is the Nazi concentration camp, Dachau. Most people think that it was in an isolated location, but it was actually in the middle of a residential neighborhood. People sat at their dinner tables every night watching what happened. While this is much different from what happens in the work-place, our reluctance to speak up when we see a violation of a person's individuality is essentially the same thing. We fear being the next victim.

- This organization is saying it is okay to speak up in an effort to create an environment which values diversity. I can't guarantee that you will always get a warm reception, but this training is a powerful statement that we want people to refrain from collusion.

00:05   **The Platinum Rule**

 REFER to the handout and overhead, The Platinum Rule (pages 188 and 281, respectively).

 ASK

- Why do you think we've focused on The Platinum Rule as the cornerstone for the diversity effort?

- How do we find out how others want to be treated?

- Is it possible to use The Platinum Rule? What might some obstacles be?

- How many people are critical to your success in your job? Would it be logistically possible to use The Platinum Rule with them?

 LISTEN for answers such as:

- The Platinum Rule extends beyond The Golden Rule by making it okay for us to have differences.

- We find out how others want to be treated by asking them.

- It might take longer to implement The Platinum Rule, and we don't have time to do it with everyone.

- It would be possible to use it with the people crucial to our success.

 SAY in summary:

- The Platinum Rule honors the differences in people.

- Realistically, we aren't able to ask everyone we meet how they want to be treated. However, if we focus on the people who are crucial to our success, maybe eight to ten people, this is very feasible. For casual contacts, such as people we pass in the hallway, The Golden Rule is still a good practice.

- The Platinum Rule also requires us to make our preferences known to others. Having the courage to speak up is a key responsibility in creating an environment which values diversity.

00:60   **Learning About Each Other**

 SAY

You're going to divide into two groups, based on a primary dimension of diversity (either gender, age, or race). The process used in this activity will help you put the Platinum Rule into practice. Each group will go into a separate room, and have 15 to 20 minutes to brainstorm the top three answers to each of the questions on the flipchart. Take a flipchart with you, and write your answers on it for presentation to the other group when you're finished.

REFER to the questions on the flipchart, Learning About Each Other (page 62).

MONITOR participants as they complete the activity, giving a 5-minute finishing time warning.

ASK for a group to volunteer to present their answers to the other group. (The trainer should become "invisible," encouraging direct dialogue between the groups.) After the first group answers the first question, ask the other group:

- How do you feel about their issues? Are they clear? Do you have any questions or reactions?

  After the first group presents answers to question two, ask the other group:

- Do you understand these? Do you think you can do them?

After the first group presents answers to question three, ask the other group:

- Will these things help you? What additional help would you want from them?

When the first group is finished, lead a round of applause for them. Go through the same process for the second group.

ASK everyone:

- How did you feel going through this?

- Was this a useful process? How could you see it being used?

- What similarities were there between the groups' answers?

- How did the process of finding common ground help bring the groups together?

LISTEN for answers such as:

- I was surprised we had so much in common.

- Even though we disagreed, I could tell they wanted to work through it and find common ground.

- Our answers were a lot more similar than I expected.

SAY in summary:

- This process is useful for both individual and group interactions. Often, we do step one and forget steps two and three. By suggesting alternatives, and taking responsibility for a positive outcome, we learn to work together to create a more productive environment.

00:30   **Giving Feedback**

SAY

- An important element in creating an environment which values diversity is our ability to give people honest and open, constructive feedback without attacking them.

ASK

- Why do we avoid giving people feedback?

- How do we feel about receiving feedback?

- If someone objected to something you did, how would you want them to let you know?

- What are some things you would *not* want them to do?

- What would make it easier for us to give feedback?

 LISTEN for answers such as:

- It's awkward to give feedback because we don't want to hurt people's feelings.

- Sometimes we feel hurt and get defensive when people give us negative feedback.

- I would want someone to be respectful of me, and not attack me or assume the worst when giving me feedback.

- If people showed they appreciated the feedback, it would be easier to give it.

CHART answers on the flipchart, Giving Feedback Guidelines (page 63).

REFER to and give people the handouts, Giving Feedback— Handout and Giving Feedback—Case Studies found in Chapter 7 (pages 225 and 226). Ask them to work in groups for 10 minutes to answer the questions at the bottom of the case studies page. They will present their solutions to the larger group.

MONITOR the groups as they complete the activity, giving a 3-minute warning.

 ASK groups to share their answers to the questions. When each group is finished, ask the other groups:

- How did they do? What else would you add?

SAY in summary:

- These criteria help us to give feedback in a constructive way which informs but does not attack the other person. This can help us to be more proactive as change agents. Remember this the next time you're confronted with a diversity conflict situation.

00:15   **Break**

Managing Diversity

Overview

The purpose of this optional segment is to help managers learn how to fulfill their role, beyond that of valuing diversity. (Note: This segment can be omitted if the audience is not made up of managers.) The main point of this segment is that managers have power and responsibility beyond that of their reports. Managers need to understand that they control infrastructures (hiring, promotion, etc.) which can be discriminatory. Diversity is not just an issue about "being nice to each other," it is dependent on bias-free infrastructures. The key skill for managers to understand and develop in this segment is role modeling. Managers often gain great insight from the activity, Manager/Employee Interview Questions.

Objectives

Upon completion of this segment, participants will be able to:

- Understand how managing diversity is different from traditional management.

- Identify the key factors for managing diversity.

- Use the Manager/Employee Interview Questions to implement The Platinum Rule with employees.

- Assess their own skills in managing diversity.

 Prepare for the activity, Key Factors for Managing Diversity, by attaching a 3-foot by 5-foot piece of construction paper to the wall. Cover the paper with repositionable mounting spray. Prepare two colored sheets in large, bold print. One says *3 to 5 words* and the other says *big, bold letters*. Stick these to the construction paper.

You will also need to place 8 1/2-inch by 5 1/2-inch sheets of colored paper in the center of each table before beginning this activity. Plan to have at least five sheets available for each participant.

Workshop Agenda

5. Managing Diversity	**Minutes** **50**	**Start / Stop** **3:05/ 3:55**	**Actual Start / Stop**
Managing Diversity Versus Traditional Management	15	3:05 / 3:20	_____ / _____
Key Factors for Managing Diversity	20	3:20 / 3:40	_____ / _____
Manager/Employee Interview Questions	10	3:40 / 3:50	_____ / _____
Managing Diversity Self-Assessment	5	3:50 / 3:55	_____ / _____

5. Managing Diversity (3:05 to 3:55)

00:15   **Managing Diversity Versus Traditional Management**

 REFER to the handout, Managing Diversity Versus Traditional Management (page 189).

 ASK people to work in small groups for 5 minutes to answer the following questions:

- How is managing diversity different from traditional management?

- What additional skills may be required for managing diversity?

- What are some reasons managers might resist managing diversity?

- What do managers have to gain by becoming good at managing diversity?

 ASK each group to share their answers.

 LISTEN for answers such as:

- Managing diversity is a process, whereas traditional management is more task oriented.

- Managing diversity is more people oriented and shows a value for the individual's contribution.

- Managing diversity requires more flexibility and communication skills.

- Managers might resist it because it seems like it might be more work, take more time, or be difficult to learn.

- Managers who get good at it will be more valuable in the marketplace.

 SAY in summary:

- Managing diversity is a process focused on creating an environment in which everyone can be equally productive.

- Several skills are required, including valuing diversity, understanding our own perceptions and biases, relating to people as individuals, and being a champion of change. Courage is also a major requirement.

- Managers who will be in demand in the future are those who are good at managing a variety of people, not just people like themselves.

00:20 **Key Factors for Managing Diversity**

TELL participants that they are going to use a process to define the key factors for effectively managing diversity. Explain that managers have a role beyond that of regular employees, because they are in positions which have the authority to influence the organization's infrastructures, such as hiring, promotions, increases, social norms, etc.

REFER people to the 8 1/2-inch by 5 1/2-inch sheets of colored paper in the middle of the table, and the question on the flipchart, Key Factors for Managing Diversity (page 63).

ASK people to work on their own for 3 minutes to list at least five or six answers to the question on the paper.

TELL people to choose their top three ideas. Tell them to work in small groups to share each person's top three ideas and choose the best three to four from the entire group. Refer to the construction paper, and tell them to summarize their ideas in three to five words, and write them on the colored sheets in big bold letters. When they are finished, ask them to stick their ideas to the construction paper.

ASK participants if any items can be grouped into pairs which are similar, for example, "Role Modeling" and "Setting a Good Example." Let participants guide this—all you do is move the papers as they direct. If a dispute occurs, the person who had the original idea has the final call. Continue until all possible pairs are formed. Ask people to name each pair, for example, "Role Modeling." Have someone write these, and number each pair (i.e., "1—Role Modeling," etc.).

Now, ask participants to review their original lists. Participants should summarize in three to five words any items that are not already posted, and write them on a sheet in big, bold letters. If people want to assign a group number to their idea, they should write this on the sheet. Collect and post the sheets, leaving unnumbered ones randomly posted.

Have people direct you in grouping the rest of the ideas until several columns are formed. This may require reviewing and adjusting the original lists.

Once all items have been placed, ask participants to review all the information and determine meaningful names for the lists. As people call out names, test these off of the group until one fits for everyone. Have someone write these on new sheets and post them.

SAY in summary:

- You now have a concise list of the (five or six) most important factors for you to act on in managing diversity. You may want to write these down, or create goals for yourself in these areas for your action plan.

00:10   **Manager/Employee Interview Questions**

REFER participants to the instrument, Manager/Employee Interview Questions (page 266).

ASK

- To what extent do you know the answers to these questions about your employees?
- How would knowing the answers help you to be an effective manager?
- How might you use these questions?
- What are some other ways managers can get to know their employees' unique needs?

LISTEN for answers such as:

- Knowing the answers to these questions would be very helpful.
- These questions would reveal a lot, without invading the person's privacy.
- This is a good way to put The Platinum Rule into effect.

SAY in summary:

- One way to use the questions is to give employees the option of answering the questions individually, as a team, or as a written questionnaire.
- Often, the answers provide managers with valuable insights. The questions also enable them to build open, positive relationships with employees.

00:05   **Managing Diversity Self-Assessment**

SAY

- Now you'll have a chance to review your managing diversity skills.

REFER to the instrument, Managing Diversity Self-Assessment (page 263).

TELL people that this is for their own use only, and ask them to review their scores and the categories.

ASK

- How do you feel about your scores?

- How do you think the people who report to you would score you?

- How can you use this information in your efforts to better manage diversity?

SAY in summary:

- No matter how good a manager a person is, we all have room to improve in managing diversity. As role models, managers must set a positive example for others in the organization.

- You may want to create a diversity goal for yourself based on any items or categories for which you scored yourself lower than you would like.

Bringing It All Together

Overview

The purpose of this segment is to help people integrate what they have learned throughout the session, and to make the transition from theory to action. The case studies are designed to give people practical experience at addressing diversity situations. The vision segment is an inspiring, stimulating summary which lets people use their creativity. The stereotypes ceremony is especially invigorating, because it is a dramatic symbol of "throwing away" our old ideas. Finally, the action plan is crucial because it encourages people to commit to transferring their learning to their everyday lives. In many ways, it is the most important part of the workshop and should be treated with the respect it deserves.

Objectives

Upon completion of this segment, participants will be able to:

- Handle a real-life case study on diversity.

- Use their creativity to develop an inspiring vision of valuing diversity.

- Identify how their view of diversity has evolved.

- Understand a realistic process for the change to valuing diversity.

- Create a personal action plan for valuing diversity.

To prepare for the first activity in this segment, Real-Life Case Studies, you will need to do the following.

Two to four weeks prior to the workshop, send the Diversity Case Study Preparation letter to participants asking them to think of a real-life situation involving diversity that they would like the group to address. When the responses are returned (one week prior to the session), go through them and select several for use in the workshop. Type and copy them for handouts.

Workshop Agenda

6. Bringing It All Together	Minutes 1 hr. 10	Start / Stop 3:55/ 5:05	Actual Start / Stop
Real-Life Case Studies or Derailment Case for Managers	20	3:55 / 4:15	_____ / _____
A Vision of Valuing Diversity	20	4:15 / 4:35	_____ / _____
Changes in Viewpoint on Diversity	5	4:35 / 4:40	_____ / _____
Learning Curve/Stages of Change	5	4:40 / 4:45	_____ / _____
Stereotypes Ceremony	5	4:45 / 4:50	_____ / _____
Valuing Diversity or Managing Diversity Action Plan	5	4:50 / 4:55	_____ / _____
Summary and Review of Goals	5	4:55 / 5:00	_____ / _____
Workshop Reactions	5	5:00 / 5:05	_____ / _____

6. Bringing It All Together (3:55 to 5:05)

00:20   **Real-Life Case Studies**
                     (or Derailment Case, depending on the audience)

REFER to the handout, Diversity Case Studies (page 238) that you have prepared, based on participant responses prior to the session. (If you are using the Derailment Case Study for Managers, refer to the instructions on page 239 in Chapter 7.)

TELL participants to work in small groups for 10 minutes to create solutions based on what they have learned during the day. (Managers can use the results from the previous flipchart activity, Key Factors for Managing Diversity, to help with their answers.)

ASK participants to answer the following questions:

- What are the top two or three issues in this case study?

- How would you address this situation, using what you have learned in this workshop?

MONITOR participants as they complete the activity.

ASK participants to share their answers. Ask the other participants to comment on and add to each group's solution. If the group consists of managers, when everyone is done, ask:

- What would you add to the Key Factors chart based on what you discovered in the case study?

- How useful were these factors in analyzing the situation?

SAY in summary:

- You can see that you've learned a lot today about how to handle diversity situations. Remember this next time a diversity issue comes up when you're on the job.

00:20   **A Vision of Valuing Diversity**

REFER people to the flipchart, A Vision of Valuing Diversity (page 63).

TELL participants to work in small groups for 10 minutes to brainstorm and create their vision of what the organization would be like if we truly valued diversity. Tell them to complete the tasks listed on the flipchart. Give them flipcharts with which to create their graphics.

ASK each group to present their vision and graphic image to the group. Then, have them list their action steps. Ask other groups if they have questions or comments.

SAY in summary:

- We all want to work in an environment where we are free to be who we are, and to be appreciated for our unique contribution. Only by working together, as a team with a common goal, can we take steps every day to create an environment which values diversity.

00:05   **Changes in Viewpoint on Diversity**

ASK participants to reflect for a moment on their views about diversity prior to the session. Then, have them think about how they view diversity now.

REFER people to the overhead, Changes in Viewpoint on Diversity (page 283).

SAY

- These are some comments from other groups.

ASK

- How has your view of diversity changed since the beginning of this workshop?

- What are your key learnings?

- What is your biggest "take away"?

SAY in summary:

- Diversity has progressed dramatically over the years, and that we need to continually remember these important points to be prepared for the workplace of the year 2000.

00:05   **Learning Curve/Stages of Change**

REFER to the overhead, Learning Curve (page 284). Gradually draw the curve on the overhead as you explain it.

SAY

- In learning any skill, we go through a learning curve. Let's use golf as an example.

- If we don't ever make a concerted effort to improve, chances are that our game will probably stay the same.

- If we spend some time with the golf pro, during the lesson our swing is perfect! But when we play our first game, it feels awkward and our score actually goes down. It's tempting to go back to our old swing.

- But if we stick with it, eventually we master it and our game improves dramatically.

- Valuing diversity is similar—stick with it, and don't be tempted to revert back when new behaviors feel awkward.

REFER to the overhead, Stages of Change (page 286). Mark an "X" on each stage as you describe it.

 SAY

- Change in organizations takes time and effort, too.

- Our knowledge increases just by reading. Attitude changes are more difficult, and sometimes take place in workshops like this. We just discussed behavior change in the golf example. Eventually, entire groups begin to change. It only takes 25 percent of the people to be change agents for a whole organization to change. Finally, the organization and even society begin to change.

- If it seems like nothing is changing, think for a moment about the dramatic changes in U.S. culture. Thirty years ago, certain people were forced to sit at the back of the bus. It sounds absurd today—which is an example of how much society really *has* changed.

00:05   **Stereotypes Ceremony**

  SAY (in a humorous, upbeat tone):

- Please stand up. We're going to have a ceremony, similar to the one the kids had in the video, "A Class Divided." Go to the flipchart of your choice, rip it off the wall, tear it up, and throw it away! If there are more participants than flipcharts, please share.

- These stereotypes are not wanted in this organization—so let's get rid of them! I want to hear ripping!

 MONITOR participants as they complete the activity. Go around with a waste basket and collect the flipcharts.

00:05   **Valuing Diversity or Managing Diversity Action Plan**

 REFER to and hand out the instrument, Valuing Diversity Action Plan (page 268) or Managing Diversity Action Plan (page 270).

 SAY

- This is the most important part of the workshop, because it is what you do afterward that really matters.

- The questions are designed to stimulate your thinking (you don't have to fill them all out unless you want to) but the most important item is the *one goal* you will commit to acting on after the workshop. Make the goal something realistic, at which you can succeed.

- You may want to use ideas you learned in the workshop, or improvement areas from your assessments, as your goals.

- Take a few minutes, and then we'll discuss them if anyone would like to share their goal.

ASK

- Who would like to share their goal?

SAY in summary:

- Your actions are the most important factor in creating an environment for valuing diversity.

- Valuing diversity is of benefit to *everyone*, because it frees us to use our inherent potential.

- If every person in this room follows through on their goal, we will all benefit from a better work environment as well as from greater productivity and teamwork, which will have a positive impact on the organization's bottom line.

- One person's actions *can* make a difference.

00:05   **Summary and Review of Goals**

REFER to the flipchart, Goals, which was previously posted.

ASK

- Did everyone achieve their goals today?

SAY

- My goal as we end today brings us back to Mrs. Elliott in the video, "A Class Divided." Remember how great those kids felt after they took their collars off? That's my vision of our workplace in this organization. Together, we can make it happen. Let's hang in there and follow through on our goals.

- Thanks for your participation, and much success in your diversity efforts.

00:05   **Workshop Reactions**

REFER to and hand out the instrument, Diversity Workshop Reaction Sheet (page 272).

ASK participants to fill them out candidly. Ask them to leave them in an envelope or on a chair at the back of the room as they leave.

Chapter Four:

A Half-Day Diversity Workshop

This chapter of the sourcebook contains the training plan for your half-day diversity workshop – ready to go "as is" or to be tailored to meet your needs.

CHAPTER OVERVIEW

This chapter is divided into six parts:
- Purpose of the workshop
- Workshop agenda
- Materials needed
- Suggested flipcharts
- Tailoring tips
- The step-by-step, one-day training plan

Purpose of the Workshop

This workshop has six overall purposes. When participants have completed the session they will:

- Understand what valuing diversity is.

- Understand why valuing diversity is important for them as individuals.

- Understand why the organization is undertaking a diversity effort.

- Be able to analyze their own perceptions on diversity.

- Be able to behave in ways which value diversity.

- Be able to create a personal action plan for valuing diversity in the workplace.

There are two major differences between the half-day and one-day workshops. First, much of the group discussion around the readings and information is shortened in the half-day workshop. To compensate for this, pre-reading is highly recommended. In addition, interactive activities have been omitted from each section. The deletions have been made equally in all sections, maintaining the workshop's ability to achieve all the objectives of the one-day session, but with less depth and experiential learning.

Workshop Agenda

1. Workshop Introduction	Minutes 50	Start / Stop 8:00 / 8:50	Actual Start / Stop
Welcome			_____ / _____
Senior Manager Kickoff	5	8:00 / 8:05	_____ / _____
Trainer Personal Story	5	8:05 / 8:10	_____ / _____
Workshop Guidelines	5	8:10 / 8:15	_____ / _____
On the Outside (With Goals)	30	8:15 / 8:45	_____ / _____
Workshop Agenda/Logistics	5	8:45 / 8:50	_____ / _____

2. What Is Diversity	Minutes 45	Start / Stop 8:50 / 9:35	Actual Start / Stop
Diversity Definition and Terms	5	8:50 / 8:55	_____ / _____
Primary and Secondary Dimensions	5	8:55 / 9:00	_____ / _____
Diversity Statistics	20	9:00 / 9:20	_____ / _____
Review of Pre-reading 1	10	9:20 / 9:30	_____ / _____
Our Organization's Plans, Commitment	5	9:30 / 9:35	_____ / _____

3. Analyzing Our Perceptions	Minutes 30	Start / Stop 9:35 / 10:50	Actual Start / Stop
How We Form Perceptions	5	9:35 / 9:40	_____ / _____
Stereotypes	25	9:40 / 10:05	_____ / _____
Break	10	10:05 / 10:15	_____ / _____
Prejudice or Excluding Others	30	10:15 / 10:45	_____ / _____
Valuing Diversity Self-Assessment	5	10:45 / 10:50	_____ / _____

4. Working Together Productively	Minutes 55	Start / Stop 10:50 / 11:45	Actual Start / Stop
Review of Pre-reading 2	10	10:50 / 11:00	_____ / _____
Learning About Each Other	45	11:00 / 11:45	_____ / _____

5. **Bringing It All Together**	Minutes 25	Start / Stop 11:45 / 12:10	Actual Start / Stop
Changes in Viewpoint on Diversity	5	11:45 / 11:50	_____ / _____
Learning Curve/Stages of Change	5	11:50 / 11:55	_____ / _____
Stereotypes Ceremony	5	11:55 / 12:00	_____ / _____
Valuing Diversity Action Plan	5	12:00 / 12:05	_____ / _____
Summary and Review of Goals	5	12:05 / 12:10	_____ / _____

Notes

- _____
- _____
- _____
- _____
- _____
- _____
- _____
- _____
- _____
- _____
- _____
- _____
- _____
- _____
- _____
- _____
- _____
- _____
- _____
- _____

Materials Needed

Following are checklists of materials recommended for the half-day diversity workshop. Except for the flipcharts, masters for the materials are found in the other chapters of this book. Flipcharts are illustrated in the next section. Unless otherwise noted:

- Make one handout and instrument per participant and send them as pre-work.

- Make one overhead transparency of each one needed.

- Prepare one of each flipchart needed.

Handouts / Pre-work

Send as pre-work: (Pre-reading 1)

☐ Our Organization's Value for Diversity, page 169 (to be customized for your organization)

☐ Diversity Definitions and Terms, page 171

☐ Workplace Trends and Statistics, page 174

☐ The History of Diversity, page 176

☐ Approaches to Diversity, page 178

☐ Advantages of Diverse Groups, page 180

☐ How We Form Perceptions, page 182

☐ Stereotyping, page 184

☐ Prejudice, page 185

(Pre-reading 2)

☐ Behavior Basics, page 186

☐ Collusion, page 187

☐ The Platinum Rule, page 188

Instruments

Use before the workshop to customize for your organization:

☐ Organizational Climate Survey, page 244

☐ Organizational Reasons to Value Diversity, page 247

☐ Organization Diversity Strategies, page 249

Send as pre-work:

☐ Diversity Statistics Quiz, page 252

☐ Valuing Diversity Self-Assessment, page 259

☐ Valuing Diversity Action Plan, page 268

Activities

☐ Workshop Guidelines, page 202

☐ On the Outside (with Goals), page 204

☐ Primary/Secondary Dimensions of Diversity, page 209

☐ Stereotypes, page 212

☐ Learning About Each Other, page 220

☐ Excluding Others, page 222 (needed if not using the Prejudice segment and video, "A Class Divided")

Overheads

☐ Diversity Defined, page 274

☐ Primary and Secondary Dimensions, page 275

☐ Diversity Statistics Quiz Answers, page 276

☐ Workplace Trends, page 277

☐ Approaches to Diversity, page 278

☐ Perceptions and Stereotypes, page 279

☐ Collusion, page 280

☐ The Platinum Rule, page 281

☐ Changes in Viewpoint on Diversity, page 283

☐ Learning Curve, page 284

☐ Stages of Change, page 286

Flipcharts

☐ Workshop Guidelines, page 104

☐ Introductions, page 104

☐ Goals, page 105

☐ "One Word," page 105

☐ Workshop Agenda, page 105

☐ Our Organization's Plans, page 105

☐ Stereotypes, page 106

☐ Learning About Each Other, page 106

Special Materials

☐ Welcome

  Senior Manager Kickoff Outline, page 47
  (to be given before the session)

☐ Workshop Guidelines, page 103

☐ Fun items: noise makers, etc.

☐ Prejudice, page 185

☐ Video, "A Class Divided"
  (optional, but recommended; see ordering
  information in Appendix)

Suggested Flipcharts

Following are visual representations of the flipcharts listed on the previous page. Details of the timing and use for each can be found in the activity guides as well as in the step-by-step training plan which follows. Items which should be written on the flipchart *before* the session are represented below in **bold type**. Examples of items you will write in *during* the session are in *italics*. Notes for you regarding the flipchart are written in plain type, in parentheses. The sequence goes left to right, then down the page.

 Remember to watch for the flipchart icon in the training plans.

Note that the flipcharts for the Stereotypes activity must be hung around the room before the session starts.

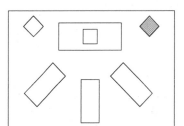 Make sure the flipchart can be readily seen from all seating locations in the training room.

Workshop Guidelines

- *Nothing we say leaves the room*
- *No personal attacks*
- *Don't interrupt people*
- *Everyone participates*
- *Be on time*

Introductions

- **Name**
- **Department**
- **Length of Service**
- **"On the Outside"— story/one word**
- **Goal, Hope or Concern**

Goals

- *Learn more about what bothers people*
- *Analyze my own biases*
- *Learn more about the company's plans*
- *Find ways to communicate better*
- *Have fun!*

"One Word"

- *Isolated*
- *Targeted*
- *Lonely*
- *Angry*
- *Demotivated*

Workshop Agenda

- **What Is Diversity?**
- **Break**
- **Analyzing Our Perceptions**
- **Lunch**
- **Working Together Productively**
- **Break**
- **Managing Diversity**
- **Bringing It All Together (end at 5:05 p.m.)**

Our Organization's Plans

(Summary of plans, based on Our Organization handout and instrument results)

Society's Stereotypes of Accountants

(You will need ten flipcharts, each with a different element of diversity. Examples may include: Asians, Working Mothers, People with Military Background, Gays/Lesbians, People over 50, Catholics, Single People, MBAs, New Yorkers.)

* Do Not Use

Learning About Each Other

- **What problems do you experience in the workplace in relation to the other group?**
- **What can the other group do differently to improve the situation?**
- **What is your group willing to do to help them?**

 The examples shown on "Society's Stereotypes of Accountants" are for illustrative purposes only. We suggest that you develop your own list of examples. To prevent the material from being taken out of context and for legal reasons, please write "Do Not Use" at the bottom of each of the ten flipcharts used in the exercise.

Tailoring Tips

The half-day workshop can be tailored in a variety of ways. The most basic level of tailoring is to include your own personal anecdotes and modify the language to fit your own personal style.

Another type of tailoring is the use or non-use of pre-work. If you decide not to send pre-work, you will either need to have people read the handouts in the session, or you will need to do longer presentations on these topics. These segments will then take longer and you will need to eliminate some of the more experiential activities. It is *highly* recommended that you send pre-work instead, but both options are possible within the half-day format.

The workshop can also be tailored in the following ways:

- Addition of examples from your environment
- Substitute other introduction / icebreaker activities
- Substitute other experiential activities
- Split it into shorter segments

Adding examples

Adding examples from your experience can greatly enhance and "bring home" important points. To do this, reflect on your own experiences and ask others for examples which demonstrate particular points.

Substituting introduction activities

If you wish to substitute other icebreakers for the one suggested, you will find two others in the beginning of Chapter 7, Learning Activities. These are My Dimensions of Diversity on page 206 and What's My Line? on page 208. They are about the same length, so the workshop would not need to be modified in any other way.

Substituting other activities

If you wish to substitute other activities, you will find many which have not been used in the half-day workshop. These are described in detail, in Chapter 3, the One-Day Workshop, Chapter 7, Learning Activities, and Chapter 5, Four One-Hour Workshops.

The Prejudice segment, which contains use of the video, "A Class Divided," is highly recommended but not required. (See the Appendix for ordering information.) If you choose not to purchase and use the video, you can substitute the activity, Excluding Others (page 222) or another activity of your choice.

Splitting material into shorter segments

If you would like to do four hours of training, but need to do it in shorter segments, you can split the design into segments that range in length from 25 minutes to 1 hour and 10 minutes. If you wish to do this, you should begin each session with a 5-minute review of the previous session, and end each session with a 5-minute preview of the upcoming session. This ensures continuity between the sessions.

Please note that the timing for the workshop as designed is very tight. If you prefer a more relaxed pace, or find yourself with a talkative group, you may want to omit an activity to allow for a time cushion.

Training Plan

Workshop Introduction

Overview   The purpose of this segment is to establish the importance of diversity to the organization, and to set a tone of openness, personal sharing, and self-directed learning for the session. You do this by being open yourself, sharing personal experiences, and building rapport with the group through interaction and humor.

Objectives   Upon completion of this segment, participants will be able to:

- Understand senior management's commitment to diversity.

- View the trainer as a role model of self-disclosure and continuous learning (rather than an "expert"), and as a diversity champion.

- Have a set of guidelines for the group in creating an environment of openness and giving each other feedback.

- Feel a sense of control and self-direction for their own learning by establishing their own goals and group norms.

- Empathize with people who are in the minority.

- Know something about all the other participants.

- Be warmed up, with everyone having shared in pairs and with the large group.

- Understand the logistics and agenda for the session.

Workshop Agenda

1. Workshop Introduction	Minutes 50	Start / Stop 8:00 / 8:50	Actual Start / Stop
Welcome			_____ / _____
Senior Manager Kickoff	5	8:00 / 8:05	_____ / _____
Trainer Personal Story	5	8:05 / 8:10	_____ / _____
Workshop Guidelines	5	8:10 / 8:15	_____ / _____
On the Outside (With Goals)	30	8:15 / 8:45	_____ / _____
Workshop Agenda/Logistics	5	8:45 / 8:50	_____ / _____

1. Workshop Introduction (8:00 to 8:50)

00:05   **Senior Manager Kickoff**

SAY that the session is starting, and move to the side of the room.

DEMONSTRATE attention to the speaker and show nonverbal support (nodding, etc.) when important statements are made.

00:05   **Trainer Personal Story**

TELL a personal story of your own learning about diversity, which demonstrates self-disclosure and that it is okay to admit we are not perfect at valuing diversity. The story should also demonstrate that you are a champion of diversity as both a business issue and as a skill which will personally benefit you in the future.

00:05   **Workshop Guidelines**

SAY

- My role is not to be the "authority" in this workshop, but is to be a guide to important information and ideas, and to facilitate our self-discovery.

- While valuing diversity is a personal decision people must make on their own, this organization also expects us to exhibit positive diversity behaviors which are consistent with the way we want to interact and do business.

- This workshop is a "laboratory" for people to test out their own ideas in relation to their peers, and that means we need to feel comfortable being open and sharing. You will get out of this session what you put in by participating.

- Disagreement is okay, and even encouraged—so long as it is done respectfully.

ASK

- What do you need in order to feel comfortable opening up and disclosing today?

SAY as an example:

- Sometimes groups want a guideline like, "Nothing we say leaves the room."

? *ASK*

- What do you think of that one?

- If someone disagrees with you, how do you want them to express their disagreement?

👥 *LISTEN* for answers that meet these criteria.

- Everyone agrees the guideline should be included.

- They are observable behaviors.

📋 *CHART* responses on the flipchart, Workshop Guidelines (page 104)

📊 *SAY* in summary:

- This is *your* list, and *you* as a group will monitor and enforce it.

- I have brought fun tools for each table (noisemakers, koosh balls, etc.), which you can use to let each other know if there has been a violation. This gives us a lighthearted way to practice being open with feedback, and also makes it okay to have fun today.

00:30   **On the Outside (With Goals)**

📊 *SAY*

- Now, we're going to do introductions, first with a partner, then for the entire group. This exercise will also help us better empathize with others who are "on the outside"–for example, someone who has an unpopular idea in a meeting, or the new person in the department.

📋 *REFER* people to the flipcharts, Introductions (page 104) and One Word (page 105).

📊 *DEMONSTRATE* by introducing yourself according to the points on the flipchart. Include both your full story *and* your "one word."

? *ASK* participants to introduce themselves to their partners, using both their full stories and their "one word."

👪 *MONITOR* the group for 5 to 10 minutes while they work in pairs.

? *ASK* for volunteers to introduce themselves and to share their "one word."

📋 *CHART* participants' goals on one flipchart, and their "one word" on another. Post them for the duration of the session.

ASK, regarding the "one word" statements:

- How would someone who was feeling these things behave at work? How would this feeling affect someone's productivity?

- What impact would it have on a team if a member felt this way?

 LISTEN for these types of answers.

- People wouldn't be very productive.

- This wouldn't create a positive work environment.

SAY in summary:

- Remembering how it feels to be on the outside can help us empathize with others.

- Think of the increased productivity and improved work environment we'd have by eliminating these feelings.

- Regarding our goals, we will (*or will not, as appropriate*) address these, and will review them at the end of the day.

00:05   **Workshop Agenda/Logistics**

REFER people to the flipchart, Workshop Agenda (page 105).

 SAY

- Here is our agenda for the day. First, we'll come to a common understanding of how we define diversity, and why it's important. Then, we'll have a chance to analyze our own perceptions. After that, we'll look at ways to work together more productively. Next, we'll talk about how to manage diversity. Then, we'll do some activities which bring all these ideas together.

- We'll end with your action plan for valuing diversity. What's important isn't this workshop; it's what you do afterward that counts.

TELL people about the day's logistics, such as break times, ending time, food provided, restrooms, telephones, etc.

What Is Diversity?

Overview

The purpose of this segment is to help people understand what diversity is, and why it is important to the organization as well as to them as individuals. Because this segment provides the most information, you need to know your facts and figures. It is also an early opportunity for people to voice concerns or questions about the topic. Participants may challenge you, and you should encourage this because it is better to have an open discussion than for people to "tune out" or let their questions go unaddressed.

A highlight of the segment is the Diversity Statistics Quiz, after which people often realize how out of touch they are with what's going on in society. The uncomfortable feelings then transition into "here's what we're doing about it," with your organization's diversity strategies. It is important to emphasize the organization's commitment in both word and action.

Objectives

Upon completion of this segment, participants will be able to:

- Use a common language in discussing diversity.

- Understand that diversity extends beyond the obvious characteristics of race and gender to include and liberate everyone.

- Test and expand their understanding of workplace demographic trends.

- Understand the history of diversity and approaches taken to address it.

- Understand that diversity is an asset rather than a burden to be tolerated.

- Understand the organization's philosophy and plans on diversity.

Workshop Agenda

2. What Is Diversity	Minutes 45	Start / Stop 8:50 / 9:35	Actual Start / Stop
Diversity Definition and Terms	5	8:50 / 8:55	_____ / _____
Primary and Secondary Dimensions	5	8:55 / 9:00	_____ / _____
Diversity Statistics	20	9:00 / 9:20	_____ / _____
Review of Pre-reading 1	10	9:20 / 9:30	_____ / _____
Our Organization's Plans, Commitment	5	9:30 / 9:35	_____ / _____

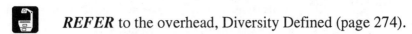

2. What Is Diversity? (8:50 to 9:35)

00:05   **Diversity Definitions and Terms**

REFER to the overhead, Diversity Defined (page 274).

ASK

- What stands out to you in this definition?

LISTEN for answers such as:

- Diversity is an asset, rather than a burden.
- Diversity includes everyone.
- Diversity is a mosaic, rather than a melting pot.

SAY in summary:

- We are defining diversity differently than you might expect. We see it as an asset to this organization, and an issue that includes and benefits everyone.

REFER to the handout, Diversity Definitions and Terms (page 171).

ASK

- What questions do you have about the definitions?

SAY in summary:

- These definitions give us a common language for discussing diversity. We will go over them in sections throughout the day.

00:05   **Primary and Secondary Dimensions**

REFER people to the overhead and handout, Primary and Secondary Dimensions of Diversity (pages 275 and 173, respectively).

SAY

- In the 1991 book *Workforce America!*, authors Loden and Rosener define diversity in terms of two dimensions: primary and secondary.
- Primary dimensions are those that we are born with. People are usually the most sensitive about these dimensions because others can tell these things about us (with the exception of sexual preference) just by looking at us. So if someone has a preconceived idea about a certain dimension, they can project that onto someone before the person even opens his or her mouth.

- Secondary dimensions are those that we have some control over, and they can change throughout our life. People also have a choice of whether they want to disclose this information or not. So people usually aren't as sensitive about these dimensions, even though these may have as big an impact on who we are as the primary dimensions do.

? *ASK*

- What additional dimensions contribute to who we are as people, but aren't listed on the chart? What would you add?

👂 *LISTEN* for answers such as:

- Family upbringing, political affiliation, lifestyle, hobbies, etc.

- Personality type as a dimension can be reinforced by saying: How many people are familiar with the Myers-Briggs Type Indicator? It's an instrument which indicates our preference for one of 16 types. If you administered it to a group of 30-year-old white men and a group of 60-year-old Chinese women, both groups would split into the 16 types. You would find that a white man and a Chinese woman who had the same personality type actually *think* more like each other than the people who share demographic similarities.

✍ *WRITE* additions on the overhead around the outside of the diagram.

? *ASK*

- Who do you think the term "diversity" is referring to?

- Are we all equally "diverse," or are some of us more "diverse" than others?

🗣 *SAY* in summary:

- Diversity extends far beyond the obvious dimensions of race and gender. People are similar and different on an infinite number of dimensions. By viewing the idea of "valuing diversity" as something that is equally relevant to all of us, it becomes inclusive as well as liberating for everyone.

00:20   **Diversity Statistics Quiz**

  REFER people to the instrument and overhead (with answers), Diversity Statistics Quiz (pages 252 and 276, respectively).

🗣 *TELL* them to calculate the number they answered incorrectly.

MONITOR people as they check their answers.

 ASK

- How did you do? Did you know as much about your environment as you thought you did?

- Are there any comments or questions on any of these statistics?

- How will these trends change the products and services we offer?

- How will the workplace be different because of these trends?

 LISTEN for answers such as:

- I didn't score as well as I thought I would. (*This is common.*)

- The workplace will be very different than in the past.

 SAY in review of the quiz and summary:

- In question number one, we can see that the workplace was created in ways which reflected the needs of the people who were originally in it. This is natural, and no one is "to blame." The problem is that the workplace has become outdated for the people who are in it *now*. (*Also see the answer sheet for other items to highlight.*)

- It is normal for people to score poorly on this quiz. It's just a demonstration that things have changed without us noticing. We need to embrace this new reality, and find ways of addressing diversity as an advantage which can enrich our workplaces and help us understand our customers better.

00:10   **Review of Pre-reading 1**

 REFER people to the handout and overhead, Workplace Trends and Statistics (pages 174 and 277, respectively).

 TELL people about the trends as indicated in the handout.

 REFER people to the handouts, Approaches to Diversity and History of Diversity (pages 178 and 176, respectively), and to the overhead, Approaches to Diversity (page 278).

 ASK

- What happened during the "Golden Rule" period?
- What did you read about the "Right the Wrongs" approach?
- Why would we now want to "Value All Differences"?

LISTEN for answers such as:

- The "Golden Rule" approach had good intentions, but didn't allow for people to be different from the dominant culture.

- "Right the Wrongs" was a step in the right direction, but created an "us versus them" mentality and split people apart.

SAY in summary:

- We have evolved as a society to the point where we now are able to see diversity as an asset, rather than a process of quota-filling. Valuing diversity is the approach we are taking in this organization.

REFER people to the handout, Advantages of Diverse Groups (page 180).

TELL people about the research highlighted in the handout.

00:05   **Our Organization's Plans and Commitment**

REFER people to the handout, Our Organization's Value for Diversity (page 169) and the flipchart, Our Organization's Plans (page 105).

TELL people about your organization's commitment and plans, as highlighted in the handout.

ASK

- What do you think this organization will have to do to make this effort succeed?

- What questions do you have about our organization's commitment before we move on to analyzing our perceptions?

SAY in summary:

- This organization has chosen to view diversity as a bottom-line issue which is an asset to our business and includes everyone. As you can see, we are truly committed to creating an environment which values diversity.

Analyzing Our Perceptions

Overview

The purpose of this segment is to help people understand how we form our perceptions, and to help them to analyze their own. This is a very important segment, in which trainers often see "light bulbs going off" in participants' minds.

The segment builds, starting with the idea that we all stereotype people and screen out contradictory facts. Then, people list stereotypes. The trainer needs to ask good questions so people discover on their own that they may be projecting inaccurate perceptions onto others; telling them is not nearly as effective. (The Stereotypes activity requires skilled facilitation, so you should review the full instructions in Chapter 7.)

Use of the video, "A Class Divided," is highly recommended but not required. You can substitute the activity, Excluding Others (page 222) if desired, or substitute another activity of your choice. (See the activity description for complete instructor information). If the video is used, during this segment people sometimes laugh (it is funny at times), or the room becomes quiet as people feel its impact. Usually, people see the dramatic impact of stereotyping and that it is often made up in our minds. This can be a turning point for people's self-realization and commitment to valuing diversity. Finally, people assess their own skills and developmental areas.

Objectives

Upon completion of this segment, participants will be able to:

• Understand how perceptions are formed and can turn into stereotypes.

• Discover how we form our perceptions.

• Identify common stereotypes and realize their negative impact.

• Assess their own skill level in valuing diversity.

 The following video is optional, but recommended for this segment:

"A Class Divided" (purchase $200, no rental available) VideoLearning Resource Group, 1-800-225-3959.

(Note that you use the first 20 minutes for the Prejudice activity.)

Workshop Agenda

3. Analyzing Our Perceptions	Minutes 30	Start / Stop 9:35/ 10:50	Actual Start / Stop
How We Form Perceptions	5	9:35 / 9:40	_____ / _____
Stereotypes	25	9:40 / 10:05	_____ / _____
Break	10	10:05 / 10:15	_____ / _____
Prejudice or Excluding Others	30	10:15 / 10:45	_____ / _____
Valuing Diversity Self-Assessment	5	10:45 / 10:50	_____ / _____

3. Analyzing Our Perceptions (9:35 to 10:50)

00:05

How We Form Perceptions

REFER to the handout, How We Form Perceptions (page 182) and the overhead, Perceptions and Stereotypes (page 279).

TELL people about perceptions as described in the handout.

00:25

Stereotypes

REFER to the handout, Stereotyping (page 184).

SAY

- Stereotypes are a necessary part of the way our brains function. We have so much data coming at us, that our brains only actually pay attention to a small percentage of it. The rest is sorted by category so we don't have to think about it. Stereotypes become negative when we filter out evidence which contradicts our preconceived ideas.

- Now we're going to do an activity which helps us identify common stereotypes, based on a variety of the primary and secondary dimensions.

- Take a marker from your table. As quickly as you can, go around the room and write a stereotype that you are familiar with on each flipchart. The only rule is that you can't repeat one that is already listed. You will have 5 to 10 minutes to do this.

MONITOR people as they complete the activity.

TELL people to take their seats and read the charts.

ASK

- How did you feel writing the stereotypes down? Why?

- How do you feel, seeing all these stereotypes?

- What percentage are negative? Why are so many negative?

- Is anyone exempt from being stereotyped?

- How does it feel to know people may be stereotyping *you* in these ways?

- What impact does it have on a person, if we perceive that person according to what is on these flipcharts?

- Does anyone know of a person (other than yourself) who doesn't fit one of these stereotypes? When we do, is our tendency to change our stereotype, or to say "they're the exception?" (e.g., "He's not your typical New Yorker.")

- Do you think these stereotypes ever creep into this organization? What would happen if they did?

 LISTEN for answers such as:

- We focus on the negative, rather than the positive in people.

- Stereotypes apply to everyone, and everyone is hurt by them.

- Maybe we see what we're looking for, instead of what's really there.

- If someone contradicts the stereotype, we usually think they're the exception rather than change our stereotype.

- Seeing these things in people is a waste of energy, and hurts our productivity.

 SAY in summary:

- It took the group only about 5 minutes to come up with nearly X number (100, etc.) of stereotypes. If we had an hour, we could come up with thousands. Stereotypes are prevalent in our society, and we need to heighten our awareness of them to keep them from influencing our perceptions of others and to keep them from distorting our view of people as they really are.

00:10   **Break**

00:30   **Prejudice (optional)**

 SAY

- Often, people wonder where stereotypes come from. We're going to watch a video called "A Class Divided." It's a PBS documentary, originally filmed in 1968, in which a teacher creates a microcosm of society in a third-grade classroom in an all-white, all-Christian farming community in Iowa. Although her focus is on racial issues, what you're about to see applies to all kinds of diversity issues. I think you'll find it pretty dramatic. It's about 20 minutes long.

 PLAY the video, "A Class Divided," starting with "Good evening. Tonight on Frontline . . ." and ending with the children hugging after they take off their collars (before the teacher is interviewed).

 ASK

- What are your reactions to this?

- Where did the stereotypes come from? How did the teacher create them?

- In applying this to society, or our organization, who or what fills the role of the teacher?

- Why do you think the "up" kids were so mean to their friends? Do we do this as adults?

- Why did the children's test scores go down? How does this happen in the workplace?

- Why did the children buy into the idea that they were in the "down" group, even on the second day when they knew it wasn't real? Do we do this to ourselves as adults?

- How do situations like the one in "A Class Divided" happen in the workplace?

LISTEN for answers such as:

- The teacher created the stereotypes by picking random examples, and then applying them broadly to the whole group.

- Authority figures such as leaders, or the media, have the same influence as the teacher.

- The kids were mean because they knew they could get away with it—it's a power game, just like that of adults.

- The children's scores went down, just like a self-fulfilling prophecy. This also happens when people at work expect the worst from us, or when we buy into others' stereotypes of us.

- This happens all the time, with "in groups" and "out groups" at work, or with people whose characteristics or ideas are different from the dominant group.

SAY in summary:

- This video shows what happens when we allow prejudice and bias into any group, including the workplace. As an organization, we can't afford such an extreme waste of energy and productivity. Valuing diversity can help us to overcome this.

00:05   **Valuing Diversity Self-Assessment**

SAY

- Now we'll have a chance to see where we are in our own ability to value diversity.

REFER to the instrument, Valuing Diversity Self-Assessment (page 259).

TELL people this is for their own use only, and ask them to review their scores and the categories.

ASK

- What do each of the scoring categories mean to you?

- In which category do you think the organization would like everyone to score?

- How can you use this information in your efforts to better value diversity?

LISTEN for answers such as:

- Naive seems like it could be in any score range, because the person is unaware of his or her behavior.

- The organization would probably like us to be change agents.

- This gives me ideas of things I can do to show that I value diversity.

SAY in summary:

- While most people fall in the Traditional or Neutral categories, the company is doing this diversity training to encourage more people to become Change Agents.

- You may want to create a diversity goal for yourself based on any items for which you scored yourself lower than you would like, and include it in your action plan.

Working Together Productively

Overview

The purpose of this segment is to help people learn new behaviors to create an environment that values diversity. The activities, Behavior Basics and Collusion, set the stage with a discussion of how and why diversity violations occur. We then move to the cornerstone of this segment: The Platinum Rule and how to use it. The activity, Learning About Each Other, is a vivid demonstration of this principle in practice, and usually has a strong impact on participants. If done well, the group will discover that it is not as hard as they thought to talk about difficult issues, and that they now have an easy format for doing so. They also usually learn something useful about the other group. It is important for you to encourage the groups to carry on a dialogue among themselves, rather than having them present information to you. The activity, Giving Feedback, provides solid practice for people in addressing diversity violations in a productive manner.

Objectives

Upon completion of this segment, participants will be able to:

- State the minimum legal requirements for diversity behavior.

- Recognize collusion, and how to avoid it.

- Describe the benefits of using The Platinum Rule.

- Communicate about difficult or taboo issues with others in an open way that values the other person or group.

Workshop Agenda

4. Working Together Productively	Minutes 55	Start / Stop 10:50 / 11:45	Actual Start / Stop
Review of Pre-reading 2	10	10:50 / 11:00	_____ / _____
Learning About Each Other	45	11:00 / 11:45	_____ / _____

4. Working Together Productively (10:50 to 11:45)

00:10   **Review of Pre-reading 2**

 REFER to the handout, Behavior Basics (page 186).

 TELL people about behavior basics as described in the handout.

ASK

- How might examples like the ones listed on your handout be interpreted as creating a biased or harassing environment?

- What other words, expressions, phrases, or behaviors have you heard which you or others might find inappropriate or offensive?

LISTEN for answers such as:

- These behaviors reinforce stereotypes and could be seen as devaluing people.

- In using The Platinum Rule, we find out whether these things bother someone or not, rather than assuming.

- Other inappropriate words might include the use of "guys" when referring to a group of people.

- Other inappropriate behaviors might include talking about sports or women's issues in a way which excludes another group, etc.

SAY in summary:

- These guidelines are the bare minimum in creating an environment which values diversity.

- The bottom line is this: Does it add value to workplace productivity? If it doesn't, and could potentially cause a problem, why do it?

REFER to the handout and overhead Collusion (pages 187 and 280, respectively).

ASK

- What kind of collusion do you think is most common?

- Why would people remain silent?

LISTEN for answers such as:

- People are afraid of being the next target.

- People don't want to risk their careers or their acceptance by the group.

SAY in summary:

- Silence may seem harmless, but it can reinforce stereotyping and a lack of value for diversity.

- An extreme example is the Nazi concentration camp, Dachau. Most people think that it was in an isolated location, but it was actually in the middle of a residential neighborhood. People sat at their dinner tables every night watching what happened. While this is much different from what happens in the work-place, our reluctance to speak up when we see a violation of a person's individuality is essentially the same thing. We fear being the next victim.

- This organization is saying it is okay to speak up in an effort to create an environment which values diversity. I can't guarantee that you will always get a warm reception, but this training is a powerful statement that we want people to refrain from collusion.

  REFER to the handout and overhead, The Platinum Rule (pages 188 and 281, respectively).

 ASK

- Why do you think we've focused on The Platinum Rule as the cornerstone for the diversity effort?

- How do we find out how others want to be treated?

- Is it possible to use The Platinum Rule? What might some obstacles be?

- How many people are critical to your success in your job? Would it be logistically possible to use The Platinum Rule with them?

 LISTEN for answers such as:

- The Platinum Rule extends beyond The Golden Rule by making it okay for us to have differences.

- We find out how others want to be treated by asking them.

- It might take longer to implement The Platinum Rule, and we don't have time to do it with everyone.

- It would be possible to use it with the people crucial to our success.

SAY in summary:

- The Platinum Rule honors the differences in people.

- Realistically, we aren't able to ask everyone we meet how they want to be treated. However, if we focus on the people who are crucial to our success, maybe eight to ten people, this is very feasible. For casual contacts, such as people we pass in the hallway, The Golden Rule is still a good practice.

- The Platinum Rule also requires us to make our preferences known to others. Having the courage to speak up is a key responsibility in creating an environment which values diversity.

00:45   **Learning About Each Other**

SAY

- You're going to divide into two groups, based on a primary dimension of diversity (either gender, age, or race). The process used in this activity will help you put the Platinum Rule into practice. Each group will go into a separate room, and have 15 to 20 minutes to brainstorm the top three answers to each of the questions on the flipchart. Take a flipchart with you, and write your answers on it for presentation to the other group when you're finished.

REFER to the questions on the flipchart, Learning About Each Other (page 106).

MONITOR participants as they complete the activity, giving a 5-minute finishing time warning.

ASK for a group to volunteer to present their answers to the other group. (The trainer should become "invisible," encouraging direct dialogue between the groups.) After the first group answers the first question, ask the other group:
- How do you feel about their issues? Are they clear? Do you have any questions or reactions?

After the first group presents answers to question two, ask the other group:
- Do you understand these? Do you think you can do them?

After the first group presents answers to question three, ask the other group:
- Will these things help you? What additional help would you want from them?

(When the first group is finished, lead a round of applause for them. Go through the same process for the second group.)

ASK everyone:

- How did you feel going through this?

- Was this a useful process? How could you see it being used?

- What similarities were there between the groups' answers?

- How did the process of finding common ground help bring the groups together?

 LISTEN for answers such as:

- I was surprised we had so much in common.

- Even though we disagreed, I could tell they wanted to work through it and find common ground.

- Our answers were a lot more similar than I expected.

 SAY in summary:

- This process is useful for both individual and group interactions. Often, we do step one and forget steps two and three. By suggesting alternatives, and taking responsibility for a positive outcome, we learn to work together to create a more productive environment.

Bringing It All Together

Overview

The purpose of this segment is to help people integrate what they have learned throughout the session, and to make the transition from theory to action. The case studies are designed to give people practical experience at addressing diversity situations. The vision segment is an inspiring, stimulating summary which lets people use their creativity. The stereotypes ceremony is especially invigorating, because it is a dramatic symbol of "throwing away" our old ideas. Finally, the action plan is crucial because it encourages people to commit to transferring their learning to their everyday lives. In many ways, it is the most important part of the workshop and should be treated with the respect it deserves.

Objectives

Upon completion of this segment, participants will be able to:

- Identify how their view of diversity has evolved.

- Understand a realistic process for the change to valuing diversity.

- Create a personal action plan for valuing diversity.

Workshop Agenda

5. Bringing It All Together	Minutes 25	Start / Stop 11:45 / 12:10	Actual Start / Stop
Changes in Viewpoint on Diversity	5	11:45 / 11:50	_____ / _____
Learning Curve/Stages of Change	5	11:50 / 11:55	_____ / _____
Stereotypes Ceremony	5	11:55 / 12:00	_____ / _____
Valuing Diversity Action Plan	5	12:00 / 12:05	_____ / _____
Summary and Review of Goals	5	12:05 / 12:10	_____ / _____

5. Bringing It All Together (11:45 to 12:10)

00:05   **Changes in Viewpoint on Diversity**

ASK participants to reflect for a moment on their views about diversity prior to the session. Then, have them think about how they view diversity now.

REFER people to the overhead, Changes in Viewpoint on Diversity (page 283).

SAY

• These are some comments from other groups.

ASK

• How has your view of diversity changed since the beginning of this workshop?

• What are your key learnings?

• What is your biggest "take away"?

SAY in summary:

• Diversity has progressed dramatically over the years, and we need to continually remember these important points to be prepared for the workplace of the year 2000.

00:05   **Learning Curve/Stages of Change**

REFER to the overhead, Learning Curve (page 284). Gradually draw the curve on the overhead as you explain it.

SAY

- In learning any skill, we go through a learning curve. Let's use golf as an example.

- If we don't ever make a concerted effort to improve, chances are that our game will probably stay the same.

- If we spend some time with the golf pro, during the lesson our swing is perfect! But when we play our first game, it feels awkward and our score actually goes down. It's tempting to go back to our old swing.

- But if we stick with it, eventually we master it and our game improves dramatically.

- Valuing diversity is similar—stick with it, and don't be tempted to revert back when new behaviors feel awkward.

REFER to the overhead, Stages of Change (page 286). Mark an "X" on each stage as you describe it.

SAY

- Change in organizations takes time and effort, too.

- Our knowledge increases just by reading. Attitude changes are more difficult, and sometimes take place in workshops like this. We just discussed behavior change in the golf example. Eventually, entire groups begin to change. It only takes 25 percent of the people to be change agents for a whole organization to change. Finally, the organization and even society begin to change.

- If it seems like nothing is changing, think for a moment about the dramatic changes in U.S. culture. Thirty years ago, certain people were forced to sit at the back of the bus. It sounds absurd today—which is an example of how much society really *has* changed.

00:05   **Stereotypes Ceremony**

SAY (in a humorous, upbeat tone):

- Please stand up. We're going to have a ceremony, similar to the one the kids had in the video, "A Class Divided." Go to the flip-chart of your choice, rip it off the wall, tear it up, and throw it away! If there are more participants than flipcharts, please share.

- These stereotypes are not wanted in this organization—so let's get rid of them! I want to hear ripping!

MONITOR participants as they complete the activity. Go around with a waste basket and collect the flipcharts.

00:05   **Valuing Diversity Action Plan**

REFER to and hand out the instrument, Valuing Diversity Action Plan (page 268).

SAY

- This is the most important part of the workshop, because it is what you do afterward that really matters.

- The questions are designed to stimulate your thinking (you don't have to fill them all out unless you want to) but the most important item is the *one goal* you will commit to acting on after the workshop. Make the goal something realistic, at which you can succeed.

- You may want to use ideas you learned in the workshop, or improvement areas from you assessments, as your goals.

- Take a few minutes, and then we'll discuss them if anyone would like to share their goal.

ASK

- Who would like to share their goal?

SAY in summary:

- Your actions are the most important factor in creating an environment for valuing diversity.

- Valuing diversity is of benefit to *everyone*, because it frees us to use our inherent potential.

- If every person in this room follows through on their goal, we will all benefit from a better work environment as well as from greater productivity and teamwork, which will have a positive impact on the organization's bottom line.

- One person's actions *can* make a difference.

00:05   **Summary and Review of Goals**

REFER to the flipchart, Goals (page 105), which was previously posted.

ASK

- Did everyone achieve their goals today?

 SAY

- My goal as we end today brings us back to Mrs. Elliott in the video "A Class Divided." Remember how great those kids felt after they took their collars off? That's my vision of our workplace in this organization. Together, we can make it happen. Let's hang in there and follow through on our goals.

- Thanks for your participation, and much success in your diversity efforts.

Notes

- _____
- _____
- _____
- _____
- _____
- _____
- _____
- _____
- _____
- _____
- _____
- _____
- _____
- _____
- _____
- _____
- _____
- _____
- _____
- _____

Chapter Five:

One-Hour Diversity Workshops

This chapter contains training plans for four one-hour diversity workshops—ready to go "as is" or to be tailored or combined to meet your needs. (Note that you can also pull one-hour segments from the one-day and half-day workshops; therefore, those segments will not be included.)

WORKSHOP TOPICS

The chapter is divided into four parts, one for each one-hour workshop. The four workshops are:

1. Valuing Diversity
2. Managing Diversity
3. Follow-Up on Conflict
4. Refresher

Each one-hour workshop includes:

*   Overview
*   Workshop Agenda
*   Materials Needed
*   Suggested Flipcharts
*   Tailoring Tips
*   Training Plan

The one-hour workshops incorporate items from Chapter 7, Learning Activities, which were not used in the one-day or half-day workshops. Therefore, the one-hour outlines can give you ideas on how to use these activities if you would like to replace segments from the longer workshops.

 Note that the introduction segments to each one-hour workshop are very brief, with the assumption that participants already know each other. If they do not, the session may need to be tailored to include a more in-depth introduction.

Valuing Diversity

Purpose

This one-hour workshop is designed as an introduction to the most important concepts of valuing diversity. It can be used with groups who may not have time for the one-day or half-day sessions, or as a "preview" held prior to the longer sessions. A drawback of this session is that it is information-intensive, focusing on lecture rather than group participation. In tailoring, this can be modified; however, any group activity will require larger amounts of time and may limit the true "overview" nature of the session.

Overview

This workshop gives people an overview of the primary issues and ideas on the subject of diversity. It is designed to disseminate information rather than to change attitudes or behavior. It helps people understand what diversity is, and why it is important to the organization as well as to themselves as individuals. A highlight is the Diversity Statistics Quiz, after which people often realize how out of touch they are with what's going on in society. We talk about collusion, and how and why diversity violations occur. We then move to the cornerstone of this segment: The Platinum Rule and how to use it. People have a chance to assess their own skills in valuing diversity. It is important to end with a strong emphasis on the organization's commitment to valuing diversity in both word and action.

Objectives

Upon completion of this workshop, participants will be able to:

• Have a common language for diversity terms.

• Understand the basic concepts of valuing diversity.

• Understand that diversity extends beyond the obvious characteristics of race and gender to include and liberate everyone.

• Test and expand their understanding of workplace demographic trends.

• Understand that diversity is an asset rather than a burden.

• Understand collusion, and how to avoid it.

• Understand the benefits of using The Platinum Rule.

• Assess their own skills in valuing diversity.

• Understand their organization's reasons for undertaking a diversity effort.

Workshop Agenda

1. **Valuing Diversity**	**Minutes** 60	**Start / Stop** 8:00 / 9:00	**Actual Start / Stop**
Welcome and Agenda	5	8:00 / 8:05	_____ / _____
Diversity Definitions and Terms	5	8:05 / 8:10	_____ / _____
Primary and Secondary Dimensions	5	8:10 / 8:15	_____ / _____
Diversity Statistics Quiz	10	8:15 / 8:25	_____ / _____
Workplace Trends	5	8:25 / 8:30	_____ / _____
Diversity History and Approaches	5	8:30 / 8:35	_____ / _____
Advantages of Diverse Groups	5	8:35 / 8:40	_____ / _____
Collusion and The Platinum Rule	5	8:40 / 8:45	_____ / _____
Valuing Diversity Self-Assessment	5	8:45 / 8:50	_____ / _____
Our Organization Plans, Commitments	5	8:50 / 8:55	_____ / _____
Summary	5	8:55 / 9:00	_____ / _____

Notes

- _____
- _____
- _____
- _____
- _____
- _____
- _____
- _____
- _____
- _____
- _____
- _____
- _____
- _____

Materials Needed

These are the materials recommended for this one-hour session. Except for the flipchart, masters for the materials are found in the other chapters of this book. The flipchart is illustrated on the next page. Unless otherwise noted:

- Make one handout and instrument per participant and send them as pre-work.

- Make one overhead transparency of each one needed.

- Prepare one of each flipchart needed.

Handouts / Pre-work

Send as pre-work:

☐ Our Organization's Value for Diversity, page 169

☐ Diversity Definitions and Terms, page 171

☐ Primary and Secondary Dimensions of Diversity, page 173

☐ Workplace Trends and Statistics, page 174

☐ The History of Diversity, pages 176

☐ Approaches to Diversity, pages 178

☐ Advantages of Diverse Groups, page 180

☐ Collusion, page 187

☐ The Platinum Rule, page 188

Instruments

Send as pre-work:

☐ Diversity Statistics Quiz, page 252

☐ Valuing Diversity Self-Assessment—Worksheet, page 259

Activities

☐ Primary and Secondary Dimensions of Diversity, page 209

Overheads

☐ Diversity Defined, page 274

☐ Primary and Secondary Dimensions of Diversity, page 275

☐ Diversity Statistics Quiz Answers, page 276

☐ Workplace Trends and Statistics, page 277

☐ Collusion, page 280

☐ The Platinum Rule, page 281

Flipcharts / Special Materials

☐ Our Organization's Plans, page 135

Suggested Flipcharts

Following is a visual representation of a flipchart listed on the previous page. Details for its timing and use can be found in the activity guide as well as the step-by-step training plan which follows. Items to be written on the flipchart *before* the session are represented below in bold type. Notes for you regarding the flipchart are written in plain type, in parentheses.

**Our Organization's
Plans**

(Summary of plans, based on Our
Organization handout and
instrument results)

Tailoring Tips

The most basic level of tailoring is to include your own personal anecdotes and modify the language to fit your own personal style.

Use of Pre-Work

Another type of tailoring is the use or non-use of pre-work. If you decide not to send pre-work and to have people read the handouts in the session, or to substitute longer presentations for the pre-work, these segments will take longer and you will need to eliminate something. It is *highly* recommended that you send pre-work instead, but both options are possible.

Adding Activities

The workshop can also be tailored by adding an activity or activities to create a two-hour or longer overview workshop. You can select from any of the experiential activities in Chapter 7 to lengthen this workshop. Reviewing A One-Day Diversity Workshop in Chapter 3 will give you ideas for activities you might want to add.

Training Plan

1. Valuing Diversity (8:00 to 9:00)

00:05   **Welcome and Agenda**

TELL a personal story of your own learning about diversity, which demonstrates self-disclosure and that it is okay to admit we are not perfect at valuing diversity. The story should also demonstrate that you are a champion of diversity as both a business issue and as a skill which will personally benefit you in the future.

TELL people about the session's purpose and agenda.

00:05   **Diversity Definitions and Terms**

REFER to the overhead, Diversity Defined (page 274).

ASK

- What stands out to you in this definition?

LISTEN for answers such as:

- Diversity is an asset, rather than a burden.

- Diversity includes everyone.

- Diversity is a mosaic, rather than a melting pot.

SAY in summary:

- We are defining diversity differently than you might expect. We see it as an asset to this organization, and as an issue that includes and benefits everyone.

REFER to the handout, Diversity Definitions and Terms (page 171).

ASK

- What questions do you have about the definitions?

SAY in summary:

- These definitions give us a common language for discussing diversity.

00:05   **Primary and Secondary Dimensions**

  REFER people to the overhead and handout, Primary and Secondary Dimensions of Diversity (pages 173 and 275, respectively).

 SAY

- In the 1991 book *Workforce America!*, authors Loden and Rosener define diversity in terms of two dimensions: primary and secondary.

- Primary dimensions are those that we are born with. People are usually the most sensitive about these dimensions because others can tell these things about us (with the exception of sexual preference) just by looking at us. So if someone has a preconceived idea about a certain dimension, they can project that onto someone before the person even opens his or her mouth.

- Secondary dimensions are those we have some control over, and they can change throughout our life. People also have a choice of whether they want to disclose this information or not. So people usually aren't as sensitive about these dimensions, even though these may have as big an impact on who we are as the primary dimensions do.

 ASK

- What additional dimensions contribute to who we are as people, but aren't listed on the chart? What would you add?

 LISTEN for answers such as:

- Family upbringing, political affiliation, lifestyle, hobbies, etc.

- Personality type as a dimension can be reinforced by saying: How many people are familiar with the Myers-Briggs Type Indicator? It's an instrument which indicates our preference for one of 16 types. If you administered it to a group of 30-year-old white men and a group of 60-year-old Chinese women, both groups would split into the 16 types. You would find that a white man and a Chinese woman who had the same personality type actually *think* more like each other than the people who *appear* to be like them.

 WRITE additions on the overhead around the outside of the diagram.

ASK

- Who do you think the term "diversity" is referring to?

- Are we all equally "diverse," or are some of us more "diverse" than others?

SAY in summary:

- Diversity extends far beyond the obvious dimensions of race and gender. People are similar and different on an infinite number of dimensions. By viewing the idea of "valuing diversity" as something that is equally relevant to all of us, it becomes inclusive as well as liberating for everyone.

00:10   **Diversity Statistics Quiz**

REFER people to the instrument and overhead (with answers), Diversity Statistics Quiz (pages 252 and 276, respectively).

TELL them to calculate the number they answered incorrectly.

MONITOR people as they check their answers.

ASK

- How did you do? Did you know as much about your environment as you thought you did?

- Are there any comments or questions on any of these statistics?

- How will these trends change the products and services we offer?

- How will the workplace be different because of these trends?

LISTEN for answers such as:

- I didn't score as well as I thought I would. (*This is common.*)

- The workplace will be very different than in the past.

SAY in review of the quiz and summary:

- In question number one, we can see that the workplace was created in ways which reflected the needs of the people who were originally in it. This is natural, and no one is "to blame." The problem is that the workplace has become outdated for the people who are in it *now*. (*Also see the answer sheet for other items to highlight.*)

- It is normal for people to score poorly on this quiz. It's just a demonstration that things have changed without us noticing. We need to embrace this new reality, and find ways of addressing diversity as an advantage which can enrich our workplaces and help us understand our customers better.

00:05   **Workplace Trends**

  REFER people to the handout and overhead, Workplace Trends and Statistics (pages 174 and 277, respectively).

 TELL people about the trends as indicated in the handout.

00:05   **Diversity History and Approaches**

  REFER people to the handouts, History of Diversity and Approaches to Diversity (pages 176 and 178, respectively), and to the overhead, Approaches to Diversity (page 278).

 ASK

- What happened during the "Golden Rule" period?

- What did you read about the "Right the Wrongs" approach?

- Why would we now want to "Value All Differences"?

 LISTEN for answers such as:

- The "Golden Rule" approach had good intentions, but didn't allow for people to be different from the dominant culture.

- "Right the Wrongs" was a step in the right direction, but created an "us versus them" mentality and split people apart.

 SAY in summary:

- We have evolved as a society to the point where we now are able to see diversity as an asset, rather than a process of quota-filling. Valuing diversity is the approach we are taking in this organization.

00:05   **Advantages of Diverse Groups**

REFER people to the handout, Advantages of Diverse Groups (page 180).

TELL people about the research highlighted in the handout.

00:05   **Collusion and The Platinum Rule**

   REFER to the handout and overhead, Collusion (pages 187 and 280, respectively).

  ASK

- What kind of collusion do you think is most common?

- Why would people remain silent?

  LISTEN for answers such as:

- People are afraid of being the next target.

- People don't want to risk their careers or their acceptance by the group.

  SAY in summary:

- Silence may seem harmless, but it really reinforces stereotyping and a lack of value for diversity.

- An extreme example is the Nazi concentration camp, Dachau. Most people think that it was in an isolated location, but it was actually in the middle of a residential neighborhood. People sat at their dinner tables every night watching what happened. While this is much different from what happens in the workplace, our reluctance to speak up when we see a diversity violation is in essence the same thing. We fear being the next victim.

- This organization is saying it is okay to speak up in an effort to create an environment which values diversity. I can't guarantee that you will always get a warm reception, but this training is a powerful statement that we want people to refrain from collusion.

   REFER to the handout and overhead, The Platinum Rule (pages 188 and 281, respectively).

  ASK

- Why do you think we've focused on The Platinum Rule as the cornerstone for the diversity effort?

- How do we find out how others want to be treated?

- Is it possible to use The Platinum Rule? What might some obstacles be?

- How many people are critical to your success in your job? Would it be logistically possible to use The Platinum Rule with them?

LISTEN for answers such as:

- The Platinum Rule extends beyond The Golden Rule by making it okay for us to have differences.

- We find out how others want to be treated by asking them.

   - It might take longer to implement The Platinum Rule, and we don't have time to do it with everyone.

   - It would be possible to use it with the people crucial to our success.

SAY in summary:

- The Platinum Rule honors the differences in people.

- Realistically, we aren't able to ask everyone we meet how they want to be treated. However, if we focus on the people who are crucial to our success, maybe eight to ten people, it is very feasible. For casual contacts, such as people we pass in the hallway, The Golden Rule is a good practice to use.

- The Platinum Rule also requires us to make our preferences known to others. Having the courage to speak up is a key responsibility in creating an environment which values diversity.

00:05   **Valuing Diversity Self-Assessment**

SAY

- Now we'll have a chance to see where we are in our own ability to value diversity.

REFER to the instrument, Valuing Diversity Self-Assessment (page 259).

TELL people this is for their own use only, and ask them to review their scores and the categories.

ASK

- What do each of the scoring categories mean to you?

- In which category do you think the organization would like everyone to score?

- How can you use this information in your efforts to better value diversity?

LISTEN for answers such as:

- "Naive" seems like it could be in any score range, because the person is unaware of his or her behavior.

- The organization would probably like us to be change agents.

- This gives me ideas of things I can do to show that I value diversity.

 SAY in summary:

- While most people fall in the Traditional or Neutral categories, the company is doing this diversity training to encourage more people to become Change Agents.

- You may want to create a diversity goal for yourself based on any items for which you scored yourself lower than you would like, and include it in your action plan.

00:05   **Our Organization's Plans and Commitment**

  REFER people to the handout, Our Organization's Value for Diversity (page 169), and the flipchart, Our Organization's Plans (page 135).

 TELL people about your organization's commitment and plans, as highlighted in the handout.

 ASK

- What do you think this organization will have to do to make this effort succeed?

- What questions do you have about our organization's commitment and plans?

SAY in summary:

- This organization has chosen to view diversity as a bottom-line issue which is an asset to our business and includes everyone. As you can see, we are truly committed to creating an environment which values diversity.

00:05

Summary

SAY in summary:

- Your actions are the most important factor in creating an environment for valuing diversity.

- Valuing diversity is of benefit to *everyone*, because it frees us to use our inherent potential. It enables all of us to benefit from a better work environment as well as from greater productivity and teamwork, which will have a positive impact on the organization's bottom line.

Notes

- _____
- _____
- _____
- _____
- _____
- _____
- _____
- _____
- _____
- _____
- _____
- _____
- _____
- _____
- _____
- _____
- _____

Managing Diversity

Purpose

This workshop is intended to be used with managers as a supplement to a workshop on valuing diversity. It can be tagged onto the end of the half-day session, used as an enhanced version of the management segment of the one-day workshop, or added as a follow-up session for managers who have previously attended the one-day session. It helps managers to understand how their role as managers extends beyond that of a regular employee in creating an environment which values diversity.

Overview

The purpose of this workshop is to help managers learn how to fulfill their role, beyond that of valuing diversity. The main point of this segment is that managers have power and responsibility beyond that of their reports. Managers need to understand that they control infrastructures (hiring, promotion, etc.) which can be discriminatory. Diversity is not just an issue about "being nice to each other," it is dependent on bias-free infrastructures. The key skill for managers to understand and develop in this segment is role modeling. Managers often gain great insight from the activity, Manager/Employee Interview Questions.

Objectives

Upon completion of this workshop, participants will be able to:

- Understand the manager's unique role in creating a successful diversity effort.

- Understand how managing diversity is different from traditional management.

- Understand the basic management infrastructures and how to use them to effectively manage diversity.

- Use the Manager / Employee Interview Questions to implement The Platinum Rule with employees.

- Be able to identify success factors and pitfalls in managing diversity.

Workshop Agenda

1. **Managing Diversity**	Minutes 60	Start / Stop 8:00 / 9:00	Actual Start / Stop
Welcome and Agenda	5	8:00 / 8:05	_____ / _____
Managing Diversity Versus Traditional Management	15	8:05 / 8:20	_____ / _____
Diversity Pre-reading Questions	10	8:20 / 8:30	_____ / _____
Manager/Employee Interview Questions	5	8:30 / 8:35	_____ / _____
Interview Questions	5	8:35 / 8:40	_____ / _____
Derailment Case Study for Managers	15	8:40 / 8:55	_____ / _____
Summary	5	8:55 / 9:00	_____ / _____

Notes

- _____
- _____
- _____
- _____
- _____
- _____
- _____
- _____
- _____
- _____
- _____
- _____
- _____
- _____
- _____
- _____
- _____
- _____
- _____
- _____
- _____

Materials Needed

These are the materials recommended for this one-hour session. Except for the flipcharts, masters for the materials are found in the other chapters of this book. Flipcharts are illustrated in the next section. Unless otherwise noted:

- Make one handout and instrument per participant and send them as pre-work.

- Make one overhead transparency of each one needed.

- Prepare one of each flipchart needed.

Handouts/Pre-work

Send as pre-work:

☐ Managing Diversity Versus Traditional Management, page 189

☐ How Managers Set a Tone for Valuing Diversity, page 190

☐ Diversity Employment Issues for Managers, page 193

☐ Team Guidelines and Communication for Managers, page 198

Instruments

Send as pre-work:

☐ Manager/Employee Interview—Questions, page 266

Activities

☐ Managing Diversity Versus Traditional Management, page 234

☐ Derailment Case Study for Manager—Handout, page 240

Overheads

☐ How Managers Set a Tone for Valuing Diversity, page 282

Flipcharts

(none)

Special Materials

(none)

Tailoring Tips

The most basic level of tailoring is to include your own personal anecdotes and modify the language to fit your own personal style.

Use of Pre-Work

Another type of tailoring is the use or non-use of pre-work. If you decide not to send pre-work and to have people read the handouts in the session, or to substitute longer presentations for the pre-work, these segments will take longer and you will need to eliminate something. It is *highly* recommended that you send pre-work instead, but both options are possible.

Adding Activities

The workshop can also be tailored by adding an activity or activities to create a two-hour or longer overview workshop. Two activities on the topic of managing diversity that have not been included in this design would be especially appropriate:

* Key Factors for Managing Diversity
  (Chapter 7, page 235)

* Managing Diversity Self-Assessment—Worksheet
  (Chapter 8, page 263)

By including these two additional activities, you would have a complete and well-rounded workshop on Managing Diversity, which is about 1 1/2 hours in length.

Experiential Activities

You can also select from any of the other experiential activities in Chapter 7 to lengthen this workshop. Reviewing Chapter 3, A One-Day Diversity Workshop will help you think of other activities you might want to add.

Training Plan

2. Managing Diversity (8:00 to 9:00)

00:05   **Welcome and Agenda**

 TELL a personal story of your own learning about managing diversity, which demonstrates self-disclosure and that it is okay to admit we are not perfect at valuing diversity. The story should also demonstrate that you are a champion of diversity as both a business issue and skill which will personally benefit you in the future.

 TELL people about the session's purpose and agenda.

00:15   **Managing Diversity Versus Traditional Management**

 REFER to the handout, Managing Diversity Versus Traditional Management (page 189).

 ASK people to work in small groups for 5 minutes to answer the following questions:

- How is managing diversity different from traditional management?

- What additional skills may be required for managing diversity?

- What are some reasons managers might resist managing diversity?

- What do managers have to gain by becoming good at managing diversity?

 ASK each group to share their answers.

 LISTEN for answers such as:

- Managing diversity is a process, whereas traditional management is more task oriented.

- Managing diversity is more people oriented and shows a value for the individual's contribution.

- Managing diversity requires more flexibility and communication skills.

- Managers might resist it because it seems like it might be more work, take more time, or be difficult to learn.

- Managers who get good at it will be more valuable in the marketplace.

SAY in summary:

- Managing diversity is a process focused on creating an environment in which everyone can be equally productive.

- Several skills are required, including valuing diversity, understanding our own perceptions and biases, relating to people as individuals, and being a champion of change. Courage is also a major requirement.

- Managers who will be in demand in the future are those who are good at managing a variety of people, not just people like themselves.

00:10   **Diversity Pre-reading Questions**

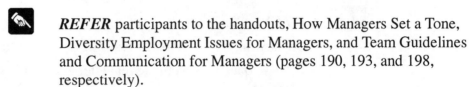 *REFER* participants to the handouts, How Managers Set a Tone, Diversity Employment Issues for Managers, and Team Guidelines and Communication for Managers (pages 190, 193, and 198, respectively).

 ASK

- Ask participants to work in pairs for five minutes discussing their answers to the questions on the handouts.

MONITOR participants as they complete the activity.

ASK

- What are some of the "managing diversity" themes that stood out to you?

LISTEN for answers such as:

- Role modeling is crucial.

- People will look to us to see if diversity is really valued here.

- We've been the victim / beneficiary of self-fulfilling prophesies ourselves.

  REFER participants to the handout and overhead, How Managers Set a Tone for Valuing Diversity (pages 190 and 282).

 SAY in summary:

- Role modeling is a manager's most important action.

- Remember the infrastructures over which you have control in creating an environment which values diversity.

00:05   **Manager/Employee Interview Questions**

 REFER participants to the instrument, Manager/Employee Interview—Questions (page 266).

 ASK

To what extent do you know the answers to these questions about your employees?

- How would it help you to be an effective manager, if you knew the answers to these questions?

- How might you use these questions?

- What are some other ways managers can get to know their employees' unique needs?

 LISTEN for answers such as:

- Knowing the answers to these questions would be very helpful.

- These questions would reveal a lot, without invading the person's privacy.

- This is a good way to put The Platinum Rule into effect.

 SAY in summary:

- One way to use the questions is to give employees the option of answering the questions individually, as a team, or as a written questionnaire.

- Often, the answers provide managers with valuable insights. The questions also enable them to build open, positive relationships with employees.

00:15   **Derailment Case Study for Managers**

 REFER to the handout, Derailment Case Study for Managers—Handout (page 240).

 ASK participants to work in small groups for 10 minutes to create solutions to the case study based on what they have learned about diversity. Ask participants to answer the following questions listed on the handout:

- What happened? What mistakes were made?

- How would you address this situation, using what you have learned in this workshop?

MONITOR participants as they complete the activity.

 ASK participants to share their answers. Ask the other participants to comment on and add to each group's solution. When everyone is done, ask:

- Do you think this could happen in real life?

 SAY in summary:

- Managing diversity takes not only commitment, but advance preparation, planning, involvement of other team members, and ongoing communication and feedback. Remember your answers next time a diversity situation comes up with an employee.

00:05   **Summary**

 SAY in summary:

- As a manager, your actions are especially important in creating an environment for valuing diversity.

- Your employees will look to you as a role model, and the organization expects you to be a leader in this effort.

- Valuing diversity benefits *everyone*, because it frees us to use our inherent potential. It enables all of us to benefit from a better work environment as well as greater productivity and teamwork, which will have a positive impact on the organization's bottom line.

Notes

- _____
- _____
- _____
- _____
- _____
- _____
- _____
- _____
- _____
- _____
- _____

Refresher Workshop

Purpose

This one-hour workshop is intended to be a refresher for people who have previously participated in the one-day or half-day workshop. It helps people to review and build on what they previously learned, both in addressing practical issues and in reconnecting with their feelings about valuing diversity.

Overview

This purpose is to help people review and build on what they have previously learned. It gives people an opportunity to cultivate a large number of practical ideas on how to value diversity. It also provides participants with an experience that demonstrates how it feels to exclude and be excluded by others. This is followed by an opportunity to think of ways to consciously include others.

Objectives

Upon completion of this workshop, participants will be able to:

- Create practical ideas with which to further value diversity.

- Remember what it's like to exclude others or be excluded.

- Demonstrate behaviors which include others.

 Have people write their ideas on an extra-large post-it note as they enter the room. (See the activity, Share Our Ideas in Chapter 7 on page 218 for details.)

Workshop Agenda

3. Refresher Workshop	Minutes 60	Start / Stop 8:00 / 9:00	Actual Start / Stop
Welcome and Agenda	5	8:00 / 8:05	_____ / _____
Share Our Ideas	15	8:05 / 8:20	_____ / _____
Excluding Others	35	8:20 / 8:55	_____ / _____
Summary	5	8:55 / 9:00	_____ / _____

Notes

- _____
- _____
- _____
- _____
- _____
- _____
- _____
- _____
- _____
- _____
- _____
- _____
- _____
- _____
- _____
- _____
- _____
- _____
- _____
- _____
- _____
- _____
- _____

Materials Needed

These are the materials recommended for this one-hour session. Except for the flipchart, masters for the materials are found in the other chapters of this book. The flipchart is illustrated on the next page. Unless otherwise noted:

- Make one handout and instrument per participant and send them as pre-work.

- Make one overhead transparency of each one needed.

- Prepare one flipchart.

Handouts / Pre-work

Send as pre-work:

☐ Reminder to bring post-it note ideas

Instruments

(none)

Activities

☐ Share Our Ideas, page 218
☐ Excluding Others, page 222

Overheads

(none)

Flipcharts

☐ Valuing Diversity, page 155

Special Materials

☐ Share Our Ideas
☐ Extra-large Post-it notes

Suggested Flipchart

Following is a visual representation of the flipchart listed on the previous page. Details of the timing and use for it can be found in the learning activity, Share Our Ideas, on page 218 of Chapter 7 as well as in the step-by-step training plan which follows. Items which should be written on the flipchart *before* the session are represented below in bold type. Notes for you regarding the flipchart are written in plain type, in parentheses.

Valuing Diversity Ideas

(Post participant's ideas for
valuing diversity on the flipchart
as they enter the room.)

Tailoring Tips

The most basic level of tailoring is to include your own personal anecdotes and modify the language to fit your own personal style.

Adding Activities

The workshop can also be tailored by adding an activity or activities to create a two-hour or longer overview workshop. You can select from any of the experiential activities in Chapter 7 to lengthen this workshop. Reviewing Chapter 3, A One-Day Diversity Workshop will give you ideas of activities you might want to add.

Training Plan

3. Refresher Workshop (8:00 to 9:00)

00:05   **Welcome and Agenda**

TELL a personal story of your own learning about diversity, which demonstrates how you continue to learn about diversity, even after having been involved in it for a long time.

ASK

- How have your diversity efforts been going since the last session?
- What successes have you had? What's working?
- What obstacles have you encountered? What's not working?

TELL people about the session's purpose and agenda.

00:15   **Share Our Ideas**

REFER people to the flipchart, Valuing Diversity Ideas (page 155). Have each participant read and explain their idea in turn while others comment. Review and reinforce the ideas, leaving them posted.

ASK

- How many people got at least one useful new idea?
- Do these spark any additional ideas in your mind?

SAY in summary:

- While it may seem like there are a limited number of solutions to diversity issues, there are actually a large number of ways to handle them. By brainstorming, being creative, and applying ideas in new ways we can find many innovative ways to value diversity.

00:35   **Excluding Others**

TELL participants they are going to work in small groups for the next activity.

ASK for one volunteer from each group.

TELL volunteers to leave the room. Explain that each group is a work team. The person outside is a new member. Say that it is *common knowledge* (be sure to use these words) that the person was only hired because he or she knew the president. Everyone has *heard* this person is not qualified, and it is likely that the rest of the team is going to have to compensate for the person's lack of skills by working harder and putting in more hours. This is the person's first day. The group is going to have a meeting in which they plan their annual party.

Go outside and tell the volunteers that they are new employees, and are going to attend a meeting with their new work team to plan the annual party. Tell volunteers that they were hired after extensive interviews and that they are well qualified, having worked in a similar job for five years. They were thrilled to be offered the job and are eager to get to work, although it is always awkward starting in a new organization where you don't know anyone. Bring them back into the room, and allow five to ten minutes for the "team meeting."

 MONITOR participants as they complete the activity.

 ASK the excluded volunteers the following questions:

- How did the group treat you? Did they exclude you?

- How did it feel to be pre-judged, and not know why?

- What techniques did you use to try to overcome any exclusion? What does this tell you about yourself?

- What verbal and nonverbal messages did the group use to exclude you?

ASK the group members:

- To what degree did you exclude the volunteer?

- Did anyone attempt to find out the volunteer's "story"?

- How far did you take your excluding behavior? What does this tell you about yourself?

ASK the entire group:

- Does this happen in the workplace?

- How important is the "grapevine" and / or preconceived ideas, and their impact on our behavior?

- What impact do they have on our productivity? Our teamwork?

TELL people to brainstorm for 5 minutes in their groups to determine ways to consciously include others.

MONITOR people as they complete the activity.

ASK each group to report back to the larger group. Each group asks questions and makes comments on the other groups' ideas.

SAY in summary:

- We can often exclude people unconsciously; but this behavior is harmful to workplace productivity.

- In the future, you may want to consciously try to exhibit behaviors which include others, and to give people an open opportunity before letting their preconceived ideas take over.

00:05   **Summary**

SAY in summary:

- Your actions are the most important factor in creating an environment for valuing diversity.

- We can create an environment which truly values diversity if each of us continues to monitor ourselves and be conscious of our behavior.

- Valuing diversity is of benefit to *everyone*, because it frees us to use our inherent potential. It enables all of us to benefit from a better work environment as well as greater productivity and teamwork, which will have a positive impact on the organization's bottom line.

Notes

- _____
- _____
- _____
- _____
- _____
- _____
- _____
- _____
- _____

Follow-Up on Conflict

Purpose

This one-hour workshop is designed as a follow-up or add-on to the one-day or half-day workshops. It enables people to build practical skills in addressing conflict, through giving and receiving feedback and assessing their own and others' conflict strategies.

Overview

The purpose of this one-hour workshop is to help people build on what they learned in a previous diversity workshop. It gives people an opportunity to receive feedback on their own "valuing diversity" behaviors as observed by other participants, and to give both positive and constructive feedback to other participants. It also provides people with ways to constructively handle conflict which often goes unaddressed in diversity situations. This is an especially valuable workshop to use with intact work teams.

Objectives

Upon completion of this workshop, participants will be able to:

- Understand how fellow participants perceived them during the previous workshop.

- Express appreciation for others.

- Give both positive and constructive feedback to others.

- Identify strategies with which to positively address conflict.

- Identify and understand people's different conflict styles.

- Use a method to constructively address diversity conflicts which often go unaddressed.

 At the end of the one-day or half-day session, you will need to have people write their feedback for all the other participants. Provide each person with a number of blank index cards equal to the number of participants. Ask people to write each participant's name on the top of one card. (Note: If participants are not an intact work team, they must have name tags or tents so that everyone knows each other's name.) Ask people to think about each person's behavior during the session and to answer the following questions (written on the flipchart). Ask them to use one card for each participant.

- What is one thing the person did which I appreciated?

- What is one thing I think would help the person grow?

Remind people to focus on behavior, not on their assumptions about each other. Collect and sort the cards, and put them in an envelope for each person. You will give envelopes to each person during the Follow-Up Workshop on Conflict.

Workshop Agenda

4. Follow-Up on Conflict	Minutes 60	Start / Stop 8:00 / 9:00	Actual Start / Stop
Welcome and Agenda	5	8:00 / 8:05	_____ / _____
Constructive Conflict	30	8:05 / 8:35	_____ / _____
Appreciating Each Other	20	8:35 / 8:55	_____ / _____
Summary	5	8:55 / 9:00	_____ / _____

Materials Needed

These are the materials recommended for this one-hour session. Except for the flipcharts, masters for the materials are found in the other chapters of this book. Flipcharts are illustrated on the next page. Unless otherwise noted:

- Make one handout and instrument per participant and send them as pre-work.

- Make one overhead transparency of each one needed.

- Prepare one of each flipchart needed.

Handouts/Pre-work

(none)

Instruments

(none)

Activities

☐ Constructive Conflict, page 229

☐ Appreciating Each Other, page 227

Overheads

(none)

Flipcharts

☐ Constructive Conflict, page 161

☐ Appreciating Each Other, page 161

  (Used during prior session when cards/feedback were gathered)

Special Materials

☐ Appreciating Each Other

☐ Name tags or tents, index cards, envelopes, pencils

Suggested Flipcharts

Following is a visual representation of one of the flipcharts listed on the previous page. Details of the timing and use for them can be found in the learning activities, Constructive Conflict and Appreciating Each Other (pages 229 and 227, respectively, of Chapter 7) as well as in the step-by-step training plan which follows. Items which should be written on the flipcharts *before* the session are represented below in bold type. Examples of items you will write in *during* the session are in italics.

Constructive Conflict

- *Don't attack the person.*
- *Discuss behaviors.*
- *Tell the person what you'd like him or her to do instead.*
- *Assume the best about the person.*
- *When receiving feedback, try not to get defensive.*
- *Thank people for giving you feedback.*

Tailoring Tips

The most basic level of tailoring is to include your own personal anecdotes and modify the language to fit your own personal style.

Adding Activities

The workshop can also be tailored by adding activities not previously used, to create a two-hour or longer follow-up workshop. You can select from any of the experiential activities in Chapter 7 to lengthen this workshop. Reviewing Chapter 3, A One-Day Diversity Workshop will help you think of activities you might want to add. By adding the learning activity, Real-Life Case Studies (page 237), you can make this workshop more specific to your organization.

Training Plan

4. Follow-Up on Conflict (8:00 to 9:00)

00:05

Welcome and Agenda

TELL a personal story of your own learning about receiving feedback and / or a conflict situation you experienced, which demonstrates how we continue to learn about diversity even after having been involved in it for a long time.

ASK

- How have your diversity efforts been going since the last session?

- What successes have you had? What's working?

- What obstacles have you encountered? What's not working?

TELL people about the session's purpose and agenda.

00:30

Constructive Conflict

SAY

- Conflict sometimes arises around diversity; but more often, we avoid conflict issues. They go unaddressed, but remain a "sore spot" for people which affects teamwork and productivity.

ASK

- Why do people avoid conflict?

- What are the sources of conflict?

- What are the positive aspects of conflict?

- What would make it easier to address conflict?

LISTEN for answers such as:

- People avoid conflict because it is uncomfortable.

- Conflict is caused by different needs, goals, values, or even miscommunication or misunderstanding.

- Conflict is positive because it helps us to become more productive and understand others' viewpoints.

- It would be easier to address if people were responsive to it.

CHART responses to the questions *below* on a flipchart.

 ASK

- How would you want someone to address a conflict with you?

- How can we demonstrate that we value someone, even though we have a conflict with them?

- How do we usually respond when someone has a conflict with us and approaches us about it?

- How could we make it easier for the person who initiates a conflict discussion with us?

LISTEN for answers like those on the learning activity, Constructive Conflict—Handout (page 231).

REFER to and give participants the learning activities handouts, Constructive Conflict—Handout and Real-Life Case Studies (pages 231 and 237, respectively) and give them a minute to read them.

TELL participants that everyone has a conflict style which affects how they behave in conflict situations.

DIVIDE people into triads. Assign a case study to each triad, and tell them to spend 5 minutes role playing the case studies with the third person acting as an observer. Tell them to take a minute to prepare, remembering the ideas on the flipchart and handout. Tell the observer to look for ways in which the role players followed the guidelines on the flipchart and handout. The observer may want to take notes during the role play. The observer also needs to determine the conflict style each person used. When the role play is finished, the observer will give feedback to the role players and the triad will spend 5 minutes discussing what happened. The observer will report back to the larger group.

 MONITOR the group as they complete the activity, giving a 5 minute warning.

ASK the observers to report back to the group, with the other triads commenting on and adding to their solutions and analysis.

SAY in summary:

- We need to be proactive in addressing conflict, always remembering to use a cooperative, "win-win" style to create an environment which values diversity.

00:20   **Appreciating Each Other**

 TELL people they are now going to receive the feedback that was collected during the previous session. Hand out the envelopes to each person. Tell them they will have 5 minutes to scan through them and think about them. They will then work in pairs for 10 minutes to discuss:

- How they feel about the feedback

- Any comments that stand out to them

- Remind people not to dwell only on the negative; encourage them to take pride in the compliments they received. Remind people that the questions answered on the cards were:

  – What is one thing the person did which I appreciated?

  – What one thing do you think would help the person to grow?

 MONITOR participants as they complete the activity, giving a 5 minute warning.

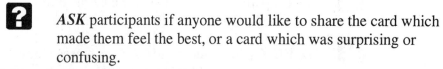 *ASK* participants if anyone would like to share the card which made them feel the best, or a card which was surprising or confusing.

 SAY in summary:

- Remember that feedback works best when we focus on behavior, not our assumptions about people.

- We often focus on the negative in others; but by focusing on and communicating the positive we help to create an environment which values diversity. We all have many positive attributes, and having them acknowledged makes us feel appreciated and included.

- We often avoid giving constructive feedback, which is a major obstacle to valuing diversity. By expressing our observations honestly and in a caring manner, and by being open to receiving feedback ourselves, we are able to bridge many differences and help each other to grow.

00:05   **Summary**

SAY in summary:

- Your actions are the most important factor in creating an environment for valuing diversity.

- Valuing diversity benefits *everyone*, because it frees us to use our inherent potential. It enables all of us to benefit from a better work environment as well as creating greater productivity and teamwork, which will have a positive impact on the organization's bottom line. Openly addressing conflict in a constructive way is an important part of valuing diversity.

Notes

- _____

- _____

- _____

- _____

- _____

- _____

- _____

- _____

- _____

- _____

- _____

- _____

- _____

- _____

- _____

- _____

- _____

- _____

- _____

- _____

Chapter Six:

Participant Handouts and Pre-Work

In this chapter of the sourcebook, you will find participant handouts for use during your workshops. The handouts are the basis of nearly all the information you will need to know on the topic of diversity. They provide the key concepts, theories, and research upon which the activities, overheads, and assessments are based. They also represent the core principles that you reinforce through comments during workshops. (You will also expand your understanding of diversity by reading additional reference material. Recommended resources are described in Chapter 2 and in the Appendix.)

HOW TO USE THE HANDOUTS

You can use the handouts in a variety of ways:

- For your own reference in preparing for presentation and discussion segments of the workshop.
- As pre-reading for participants to complete before the session.
- As handouts for participants to read during the session.
- As handouts for participants to take with them for later reference.

It is recommended that you become familiar with handouts you distribute and use their contents as the basis for any presentation or discussion segments of the workshop to ensure consistency. You will notice in the workshop guides that presentation segments last only about five minutes. They are intended to prompt discussion rather than as one-way communication. The step-by-step workshop guides in Chapters 3, 4, and 5 include questions designed to draw out participants' understanding of the material. You can then fill in any areas the participants miss during the discussion.

 We strongly recommend that you send the handouts as pre-reading, to give participants the opportunity to reflect before the workshop. With a topic such as diversity, this is especially important because people may need to reexamine their long-held beliefs.

The handouts can be sent together in a comb-bound or spiral-bound notebook with a nice cover (see Chapter 2, Workshop Preparation) for people to complete and bring to the seminar. You can also include any other pre-work, such as self-assessments or instruments, in this packet.

All of the handouts that follow are ready to be used "as is," except for the first one (Our Organization's Value for Diversity, page 169.) You will need to customize this handout to reflect your organization's diversity strategy and plans. (See the customized sample in Chapter 2, Workshop Preparation, page 43.)

Notes

- _____
- _____
- _____
- _____
- _____
- _____
- _____
- _____
- _____
- _____
- _____
- _____
- _____
- _____
- _____
- _____
- _____
- _____
- _____
- _____
- _____
- _____
- _____

Our Organization's Value for Diversity

This organization has launched a new and exciting effort to help us to achieve our business goals now and in the future. Our goal to create an environment which truly values diversity comes from our desire to make the most of trends in the marketplace and work-force.

This is consistent with high market pressures, fierce competition, and our need to increase our efficiency. Many studies have demonstrated that those companies who value diversity as part of their core business values and processes consistently are more innovative, are more attuned to the marketplace and workforce, and have a more productive team environment. You will learn more about this when you participate in our diversity workshop.

After doing extensive research, we are convinced that this effort will have a positive bottom-line impact in helping us achieve our business goals. In our research, we first looked at the unique elements of our organization which prompted us to pay attention to the issue of diversity. The key ones for us were to:

- Adapt to population statistics of *Workforce 2000*.

- Better understand our customers.

- Compete for the best employees.

- Foster innovation and well-rounded perspectives on decisions.

- Support organizational goals.

- Understand other organization's cultures during mergers.

- Reduce legal or affirmative action problems.

- Reduce conflict among diverse groups of employees.

- Support our organization's values.

- Do the right thing.

- (Other)_____

 You will need to customize this handout to reflect your organization's unique situation and outcomes of the research you conducted to customize this program. See Chapter 3, Workshop Preparation for an example.

Our Organization's Value for Diversity, (continued)

Next, we did an organizational climate survey to determine where we are now in relation to where we want to be. We uncovered some strengths to build upon, as well as some obstacles to overcome. Both are listed below:

Strengths to Build Upon   **Obstacles to Overcome**

_____   _____

_____   _____

_____   _____

_____   _____

Many of you participated in this study—thanks for your input. We have determined several ways to use these strengths and overcome these obstacles, which you will hear more about in the workshop.

We also assessed the key infrastructures which need to be in place to make this effort succeed. It is not enough for people to just "be nicer to each other"; the organization needs to update outmoded systems which may hinder the effort. As such, we examined:

- Recruiting
- Performance management
- Compensation
- Benefits
- Communication
- Events
- Training and education

In the workshop, you'll find out more about how we did in our assessment, as well as our plans for expanding and enhancing some of these infrastructures in the future.

Our organization is committed to creating an environment which truly values the unique contributions of all our employees and recognizes the diverse needs of our customers. We are prepared to "walk the talk" not only through workshops, but through the business processes that really make this organization run.

We know you will find this diversity workshop informative, engaging, and thought-provoking. If you have any questions, comments, or ideas on this effort prior to or after the session, please contact:

_____

name   telephone

Diversity Definitions and Terms

Affirmative Action   Affirmative action was created to ensure that employers took positive steps to attract, promote, and retain women and minorities if they were underrepresented in the company's workforce. This legislation was forced onto employers, and came to be viewed as "quota filling." While it was a necessary step, it created an "us versus them" mentality.

Americans with Disabilities Act   The Americans with Disabilities Act, passed in 1989, requires employers to make "reasonable accommodations" in employing people with job-related limitations. The main impact is on selection and job descriptions in employment, and in modifying facilities for buildings and retail outlets. This law applies to 43 million people, including those with HIV and AIDS, as well as many older people.

Backlash   Backlash occurs when people feel they have something to lose by valuing diversity. Programs such as "quota filling" and diversity efforts that blame certain groups for past injustices, create a "win lose" situation in which the targeted group resists and can even sabotage the effort.

Collusion   Collusion is cooperation with others, knowingly or unknowingly, to reinforce stereotypical attitudes, prevailing behaviors, and norms. (Loden and Rosener, *Workforce America!*, 1991)

Diversity   Diversity is the mosaic of people who bring a variety of backgrounds, styles, perspectives, values, and beliefs as assets to the groups and organizations with which they interact.

Equal Employment Opportunity (EEO)   Equal Employment Opportunity legislation was enacted to prohibit discrimination on the basis of race, color, religion, sex, national origin, age, disability, or veteran status. It has since been updated to include sexual orientation. EEO attempted to provide applicants and employees with equitable treatment in an organization's human resources practices, including recruitment, hiring, training, compensation, and promotion.

Ethnocentrism   Ethnocentrism is the belief that one's own group is inherently superior to all others.

Gender   This refers to whether a person is male or female. It is preferable to the term "sex," which can have other meanings. It is not related to sexual orientation (see that definition).

Diversity Definitions and Terms, (continued)

**Minorities/
people of color**

People who are not Caucasian/white. The term "people of color" is gaining popularity for several reasons. First, the word "minority" is becoming obsolete with the new demographics of *Workforce 2000*. In some states, the minority is becoming the majority. Second, other minority groups exist, including the disabled, older people, etc., so being specific about the type of minority group provides greater clarity. The term "minority" no longer refers to women, as women now comprise about 50 percent of the work force.

Prejudice

Prejudice is the tendency to see differences as weaknesses.

Sexual harassment

Sexual harassment is the use of power to intimidate others from a sexual standpoint. The courts are making awards in favor of an increasing number of sexual harassment claims, including both women and men.

Sexual orientation

Refers to a person's preference for heterosexual ("straight") or homosexual (gay / lesbian) relationships.

Stereotype

A stereotype is a fixed and distorted generalization made about all members of a particular group. It is a rigid judgment which doesn't take into account the here and now. (Loden and Rosener, *Workforce America!*, 1991)

**Traditional/
nontradional
employee**

The people who have traditionally been in the workplace—or in a particular job—are "traditional" employees. Often, this refers to white men because the workplace has traditionally been populated by this group. However, in a particular job, "traditional" employees may be a different demographic group (example: women rather than men as nurses and secretaries). "Nontraditional" employees are the people who have not traditionally been in the workforce, or in a certain type of job.

Workforce 2000

Workforce 2000 was a landmark study commissioned by the U.S. Department of Labor in 1987 to determine what the composition of the American workforce would be in the year 2000. Because the results were so dramatic, many employers took a "wait and see" attitude initially. But as the predictions started coming true, more and more companies decided to pay attention to the growing diversity of the workforce and marketplace.

Primary and Secondary Dimensions of Diversity

A crucial mistake many people make is to equate diversity with "culture." They think diversity is about "what Asians are like" or "what women want." This approach is inherently flawed because it reinforces stereotypes, which is something we are attempting to overcome by valuing diversity. This approach reinforces an "us versus them" mentality.

Valuing diversity extends beyond culture to include all the Primary and Secondary Dimensions diagrammed below. This model vividly demonstrates that we are all similar and different on an infinite number of dimensions. Culture is only one of them.

Primary and Secondary Dimensions of Diversity

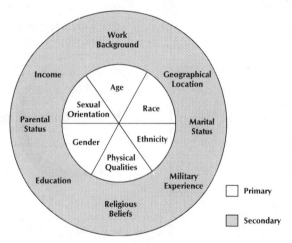

Loden and Rosener, *Workforce America!*, 1991

Primary dimensions are aspects of ourselves which we cannot change. They are things people know about us before we even open our mouths, because they are physically visible (except sexual orientation). When people feel they are being stereotyped based on a primary dimension, they can be very sensitive about it. People are usually less sensitive about secondary dimensions, because they are elements we have some power to change. We also have the choice of whether to disclose this information or not; we can conceal it.

Think about which dimensions have the most impact on you as a person. Sure, the primary ones are important. But aren't we just as influenced by where we live, whether we're married or not, and our financial situation? The primary and secondary dimensions take diversity beyond "culture," by helping us to perceive each other's uniqueness based on the many dimensions which *really* make up who we are.

Workplace Trends and Statistics

The population of America's workforce is changing rapidly. Many surprising projections rocked the business world in a landmark study called *Workforce 2000*, which was commissioned by the U.S. Department of Labor and conducted by the Hudson Institute in 1987. The most significant major trends in the U.S. population are:

- Decreasing percentages of white people.

- Increasing percentages of people of color.

- Decreasing birth rates.

- Increasing percentages of people in their middle and older years.

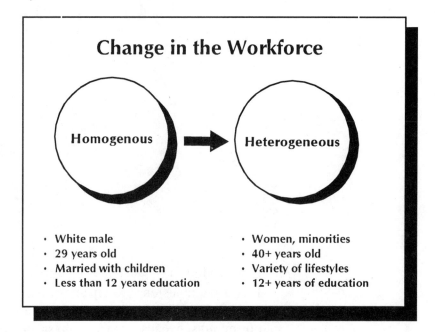

This translates into these significant trends in the workforce:

- An equal balance of men and women.

- Shrinking numbers of whites and increasing numbers of people of color.

- Most *new entrants* to the workforce will be women or people of color (85 percent by the year, 2000).

- A shortage of new entrants to the workforce under age 24.

- An increasing percentage of people aged 35 to 55 and older.

Workplace Trends and Statistics, (continued)

The bottom line is that the workplace is not the way it used to be. It is not 1965, when the typical workplace was made up of a homogeneous group of married white men, who are 29 years old, have less than twelve years of education, and have wives and children at home. The workplace is now a mix of colors, ages, lifestyles, values, and ways of perceiving the world. However, the workplace is still structured for the historical, homogeneous group.

People in the historical, homogeneous group created the American workplace based on their own similar backgrounds, styles, perspectives, values, and beliefs. When it reflected their values, this structure worked well for those who were in it. However, the structures created for a homogeneous workplace do not accommodate the majority of the workforce today. In 1992, 52 percent of working adults were women, and 11 percent of the men were minorities, which means only *37 percent* of working adults were white males—and the percentage is decreasing! It just makes good business sense to reexamine a situation in which 63 percent of the workforce may be less productive than they could be because they work in an outdated system.

It is understandable that white men created a system which worked for them, since they were the primary participants in the system. Unfortunately, the people who created the system are often labeled as "the bad guys" when the system needs to be updated. Ann Morrison, author of the 1992 book *The New Leaders: Guidelines on Leadership Diversity in America*, refers to white men as "traditional" employees, and everyone else as "nontraditional" employees. These terms encourage a new way of thinking which centers on creating a tradition of valuing everyone, without placing blame.

Traditional employees need to ask themselves: Will I cling to the old system which is becoming obsolete, or will I adapt and become successful in the new system? Nontraditional employees need to ask themselves: Will I focus on blaming the old system, or will I become a positive agent for change in the new system? It's up to all of us, as a team, to create a new system that works equally well for everyone.

The History of Diversity

To understand diversity from a contemporary perspective, it is helpful to briefly review the history of diversity in the American workplace over the last 30 years. Several governmental initiatives have been enacted with regard to diversity. Among them are the following:

- Civil Rights Act
- Affirmative Action
- Equal Employment Opportunity
- Sexual harassment
- Americans with Disabilities Act

Civil Rights Act

Think back to what America was like in the early 1960s. The human rights movement was under way. Schools had been desegregated in 1959. Many America youths were into communes, peace, free love, drugs, and rock music. Dr. Martin Luther King, Jr. and John F. Kennedy were America's heroes. Things were changing. In 1964, the *Civil Rights Act* was passed. It was the beginning of a wave of social change that continues through today.

Affirmative action

Shortly after, *affirmative action* legislation was enacted. Its intent was to ensure that employers took positive steps to attract, promote, and retain women and minorities if they were underrepresented in the company's workforce. This legislation was forced onto employers, and came to be viewed as "quota filling," which sometimes created animosity between groups. While affirmative action was not the final solution, it *was* a necessary step appropriate for the time.

Equal Employment Opportunity

Then, *Equal Employment Opportunity* legislation was enacted to prohibit discrimination on the basis of race, color, religion, sex, national origin, age, disability, or veteran status. It has been updated to include discrimination based on sexual orientation. EEO attempted to provide applicants and employees with equitable treatment in companies' human resources practices, including recruitment, hiring, training, compensation, and promotion. The Equal Employment Opportunity Commission is now responsible for monitoring and enforcing legislation regarding workplace diversity.

Sexual harassment

Sexual harassment became a focus of businesses in the 1980s and '90s. As more women entered the workforce, incidents of sexual intimidation on the job increased. Research has shown that a large percentage of women report having experienced some sort of sexual harassment. With recent publicity in this area, the courts are making awards on an increasing number of claims.

The History of Diversity, (continued)

Americans with Disabilities Act

The most recent human rights legislation was the passing of the *Americans with Disabilities Act* in 1989, which applies to 43 million Americans. ADA requires that employers make "reasonable accommodations" in employing people with job-related limitations. The main impact is on selection and job descriptions in employment, and in modifying facilities for buildings and retail outlets. This law includes people with HIV and AIDS, as well as many older people.

Notes

- _____
- _____
- _____
- _____
- _____
- _____
- _____
- _____
- _____
- _____
- _____
- _____
- _____
- _____
- _____
- _____
- _____
- _____
- _____
- _____
- _____
- _____

Approaches to Diversity

How have people and organizations tried to create an environment which values diversity? Since the 1960s, three approaches have been taken:

The Golden Rule

This approach asserted that treating everyone the same was the best solution: "Treat others as you want to be treated." Good intentions of not treating other people poorly were behind this. However, the dominant culture assumed that everyone wanted to be treated according to its traditional standards. There was no room for recognizing individual differences. It assumed that "everyone I meet wants to be treated the way I do," which is not accurate.

Right the wrongs

This approach took the form of affirmative action. "We don't have enough minorities or women—we'd better hire some, to make up for all these years of negligence." This approach created a backlash, because traditional employees felt they would be overlooked just so "a quota could be filled." It created an "us versus them" mentality, which is productive for no one.

Value all differences

This approach recognizes differences and acknowledges that they exist, but doesn't require that people be assimilated into the dominant culture. It allows for the individual mosaic of people to create one picture of an organization. It also incorporates recent social science research which has revealed that diversity can be beneficial to organizations.

Although affirmative action was well-intentioned, it focused on creating a "special" process for certain people, which was unnatural and forced. Affirmative action did nothing to fix obstacles in the system. Even worse, it created a separate employment system for women and minorities which created an "us versus them" mentality. For true equality to happen, there needs to be a *lack* of focus on race, gender, and other differences, and an increased focus on a person's *capabilities* and on system adjustments that support diversity. Only this approach will create a process which is *naturally* equal for everyone.

As Dr. R. Roosevelt Thomas, author of *Beyond Race and Gender,* wrote in a 1990 *Harvard Business Review* article:

What managers fear from diversity is a lowering of standards, a sense that 'anything goes.' Of course, standards must not suffer. In fact, competence counts more than ever. The goal is to manage diversity in such a way as to get from a diverse workforce the same productivity that we once got from a homogeneous workforce. The diversity I'm talking about is not only race, gender, creed, and ethnicity, but also age, background, education, function, and

Approaches to Diversity, (continued)

personality differences. The objective is not to assimilate minorities and women into a dominant white male culture, but to create a dominant heterogeneous culture.

Diversity then becomes equally as valuable to traditional employees, because it gives them the freedom to break out of the stereotypes they have been forced to conform to. As diversity consultant Elsie Cross has observed during workshops, "White men are oppressed by having to become clones, pressured to fit a mold—in appearance, management style, speech and behavior." (White, *Los Angeles Times Magazine*, 1992) So diversity is a liberation for *everyone*, not just women and minorities.

- Why do you think people are now refusing to assimilate into the dominant culture, when assimilation used to be the norm?

Notes

- _____
- _____
- _____
- _____
- _____
- _____
- _____
- _____
- _____
- _____
- _____
- _____
- _____
- _____
- _____
- _____
- _____

Advantages of Diverse Groups

When the statistics from *Workforce 2000* were first released, employers were shocked. Many adopted a "wait and see" attitude. Now, companies are starting to see that *Workforce 2000* trends are visible in *today's* workforce. Organizations that lead in their fields are paying attention to diversity because it's good business. Research shows there are many proven advantages of diverse groups.

Why would companies invest large amounts of time and energy in diversity? Research consistently indicates that diversity is actually an *asset* to companies, rather than just "a burden to be tolerated." In research done for the 1992 book *The New Leaders* by Ann Morrison, twelve companies were selected as models of diversity based on their efforts to institute long-term company-wide changes in transforming the dominant homogeneous culture into a heterogeneous culture. Of these twelve, eleven were later found to be included in *Fortune* magazine's list of most admired companies, with 80 percent in the top 20 percent of the list. Three of these companies won the national Malcolm Baldridge Award for quality. Companies who are making the commitment to diversity include Pacific Bell, Digital Equipment Corp., Apple Computer, Corning, Xerox, Levi Strauss, Motorola, Ford Motors, and Procter & Gamble.

Social psychologist Irving Janis studied the dynamics of a number of poor decisions made by national advisory committees, including Pearl Harbor, the Bay of Pigs, and the Challenger Space Shuttle disaster. He discovered the decisions suffered from "groupthink," which occurs when teams of similar people stifle criticism and contradictory opinions in favor of maintaining group cohesion. (Janis, *Victims of Groupthink*, 1972)

In a study by the Goodmeasure consulting group, headed by well-known management expert Rosabeth Moss Kanter, research indicated that differences in perspectives and assumptions were one of the most important factors for team success. Companies which were more innovative tended to have more women and minorities, and were also more financially successful. (K. Esty, *Executive Excellence*, January 1988)

Advantages of Diverse Groups, (continued)

In another study, researcher Carol Kovaks found that team effectiveness depends on either their homogeneity, or their ability to become productively heterogeneous. Since homogeneity is no longer the reality in the workplace, companies must choose between unproductive heterogeneity, or expending the effort to ensure that heterogeneous groups *are* productive. The reward for valuing diversity is an even *higher* level of productivity than was possible before with the homogeneous group.

**Homogeneous and Heterogeneous
Work Group Productivity**

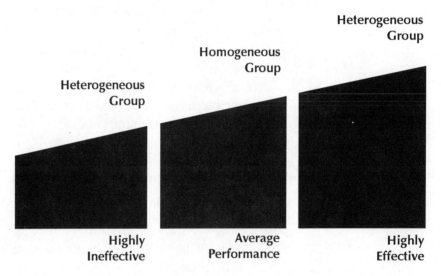

In another surprising study at the University of California at Berkeley, professor of organizational behavior, Margaret Neale, studied differences between heterogeneous and homogeneous groups. While they found that greater diversity in groups produced more conflict and subsequently more idea generation, these groups unexpectedly experienced *less* emotional conflict. Neale summarized by saying "It may take longer to get the project started using more diverse work groups, but the quality of the results can be much higher."

While heterogeneity alone is not a guarantee of a productive workforce, research has consistently shown that it positively impacts creativity, innovation, and team productivity—*if* people can transcend and value their differences.

How We Form Perceptions

Social psychologists have found that our perceptions of the world are formed to a large extent when we are children. Our families, friends, schools, and communities have a tremendous impact on who we are as adults. Often, we are unaware of the perceptions we have adopted, and accept them as "facts" without ever questioning their validity.

As Loden and Rosener point out in their 1991 book, *Workforce America!*, most of our perceptions are formed by associating with people who are similar to us in race, ethnicity, socioeconomic status, income, education, lifestyle, etc. We also tend to "cluster" with friends of our own gender. Often, the workplace is the first experience people have of being immersed in a diverse environment. Often, our opinions of people who are different from us have never been exposed to contradicting evidence. Our assumptions are rarely challenged, so we assume they must be correct. We even have the tendency to *reinforce* our existing opinions by unintentionally *screening out* contrary information.

This causes us to:

- *Magnify* the similarities between ourselves and people like us.

- *Diminish* the similarities between us and people who seem different.

- *Magnify* the differences between ourselves and people who seem different.

- *Diminish* the differences between ourselves and people like us.

The result is that we gravitate *toward* people who seem like us, and *away from* people who seem different.

In reality, even people who *seem* like us are very different in many ways, as demonstrated by assessment tools such as the Myers-Briggs Type Indicator.

How We Form Perceptions, (continued)

The following exercise may help you to find differences in someone you think is very similar to you, and similarities in someone
who seems different from you. Think about someone who is like
you in gender and/or race. How is the person different from and
similar to you? Think about things like the person's communication
style, what motivates the person, and the person's manner of relating to others.

Similar person: **Differences**   **Similarities**

_____   _____

_____   _____

_____   _____

_____   _____

_____   _____

_____   _____

_____   _____

Now, think about someone who is not like you in gender and / or
race. How is the person different from and similar to you?

Different person: **Differences**   **Similarities**

_____   _____

_____   _____

_____   _____

_____   _____

_____   _____

_____   _____

_____   _____

The point is, we are all *unique*, even if we appear to be very similar
on the outside. People who may *appear* to be similar could be very
different in terms of learning, human relations, motivation, and
communication. However, we rarely think about this or question
the perceptions we adopted as children.

Stereotyping

The generalizations we form growing up are often referred to as *stereotypes*. Generalizing is a useful and unavoidable mental process. We have so much information coming at us, all the time, that we need methods of simplifying. Our brains substitute a few categorical labels for complex masses of data. Unfortunately, stereotyping can block accurate perception of a person or event. We see someone who fits a "category" and, no matter what information is available to our senses, contradictory evidence is screened out. A *stereotype*, then, is defined as:

> A fixed and distorted generalization made about all members of a particular group; a rigid judgment which doesn't take into account the here and now.
> (Loden and Rosener, *Workforce America!*, 1991)

- What groups do you belong to?

- List some positive aspects of one of these groups.

- What stereotypes do people outside your group project onto your group?

- What stereotypes do people in your group project onto people outside the group?

Test your own gut-level reactions. Imagine the following scenario. You get on the elevator at work. You are the only person in the elevator. It stops two floors before yours, and a large black man in a long coat steps in. How do you feel, without even thinking, in this situation?

- How would your reaction be different if the person was a severely disabled woman in a wheelchair?

Prejudice

In its most unproductive form, stereotyping can lead to *prejudice,* which we will define as:

> The tendency to see differences as weaknesses.

Often, prejudice takes the form of *ethnocentrism*—the belief that one's own group is inherently superior to all others.

Although America was founded on the principle of "liberty and justice for all" and most people want to believe in equal rights, current studies show that 10 to 20 percent of Americans still express bigotry. However, there is a trend toward not openly expressing prejudice, but *subliminally* still viewing nontraditional employees as less competent. (Dovido, *The Subtlety of Racism*, 1993)

Still, studies show that even people who *want* to avoid bias are *conditioned* for a biased response. In one experiment, executives were given resumes and photos of job applicants and asked to describe jobs they might offer the people. All the resumes were identical, but the pictures were different: a white man, a black man, an Hispanic man, a black woman, and an Hispanic woman. White executives typically assigned administrative tasks to the women of color and line tasks to the men of color. Yet prejudice is so pervasive, that when women of color were given the same resumes and photos, they made the *same job assignments*. (Morrison, *The New Leaders,* 1992)

We are *all* raised with biases. One study identified that biased behavior is largely unconscious. People who display negative nonverbal reactions to others are usually unaware they are doing so. (Bass, "Bias Below the Surface," *The Washington Post,* 1990). One of the most devastating aspects of prejudice is that people deny they have biases. Denying it only perpetuates the problem.

Thomas Cummins, diversity development director at Monsanto, said that in his organization people often deny their biases because they feel "out of control." "It's the same thing that prevents me from asking directions when I get lost driving. I don't want to admit to myself that I'm lost, and I certainly don't want to admit it to a stranger." (Cummins, *Trading Places at Monsanto*, 1993)

Sometimes there is also a "backlash" of prejudice when diversity programs are perceived as quota filling. People begin to resent efforts to create a heterogeneous workforce and consciously or unconsciously undermine diversity efforts.

Behavior Basics

The basic minimum requirements for effective communication in the workplace are those dictated by employment laws enacted by the federal government. To ensure that your communication is not violating the law, rid it of any discrimination, intimidation, or harassment toward people on the basis of race, color, religion, gender, national origin, age, disability, marital status, veteran status, or sexual orientation.

The following are a few examples of words or behaviors that are not in themselves illegal but which, when combined, can create an atmosphere of bias:

- Calling someone "girl" when the person is a woman.

- Calling someone "kid" when the person is an adult.

- Expecting women to take notes and handle food arrangements.

- Expecting men to carry things and move furniture.

- Asking someone if a co-worker is gay or lesbian.

Not only can violations of employment laws cost the organization large sums of money, but lawsuits have been filed and won against *individuals themselves*. Individual behavior jeopardizes the organization. More importantly, diversity violations are unprofessional and indicate a lack of respect for what the organization stands for—no matter how harmless or humorous they may seem to the perpetrators.

While most people are astute enough not to do things that are blatantly discriminatory, the courts are now making awards for cases in which the overall "environment" indicates discrimination. This means that small, seemingly insignificant incidents, when combined together, constitute an atmosphere of discrimination.

Words, expressions, phrases, or behaviors that are judgmental, outdated, inaccurate, or inappropriate in the business environment should be eliminated from common use. Why use a word or behavior which is potentially offensive, when we have alternatives which are "safe"?

- What other words, expressions, phrases, or behaviors have you heard that you or others might find inappropriate or offensive?

Collusion

Blatant bias is becoming a rarity in the contemporary workplace. Most people have enough common sense not to publicly violate the law. However, a much more common (and often unconscious) form of exclusion occurs regularly—*collusion.* Collusion is defined as:

> Cooperation with others, knowingly or unknowingly, to reinforce stereotypical attitudes, prevailing behaviors, and norms.
> (Loden and Rosener, *Workforce America!,* 1991)

Collusion is common because of the way we are socialized as children. We all had to modify our own behavior to "fit in" to expectations of parents, teachers, friends and society. We became accustomed to ignoring our true opinions and needs as a way of increasing our sense of belonging and reducing the risk of being an "outsider." As adults, we are now able to make our own decisions about what we do and do not believe, and how to act on those decisions, rather than continuing the habit of "fitting in." There are three types of collusion: silence, denial, and active cooperation.

Silence

Silence is the most common form of collusion. By saying nothing when people tell jokes, exclude others, or exhibit other inappropriate behavior, we reinforce the "status quo." This is one reason for having diversity training and education—so that people will feel more free to speak up.

Denial

Denial sounds like a passive form of collusion, but it is actually the active stance that "no inequality exists here." After reading the statistics, or even looking at U.S. society in general, it is difficult to support the opinion that *any* organization is totally free of discrimination. Usually, people who participate in collusion by denial are either avoiding the painful prospect that inequality exists, or they feel they have something to loose by acknowledging it.

Active cooperation

Active cooperation can take several forms, some of which can be very subtle. Laughing at inappropriate jokes is active cooperation. Agreeing that "so-and-so just got that promotion because they filled a quota" is active cooperation. Participating in exclusionary networking activities (golf, dinners, etc.) is active cooperation. Men and women habitually fall into traditional male and female roles in active cooperation.

- List one or more other examples of collusion that can prevent the workplace from being equally as productive for everyone.

The Platinum Rule

A good starting point for valuing diversity is to view *everyone* as different from us, and to view them as people about whom we can't make assumptions. Appearances are deceptive; people who appear to be very similar to us are often different, and those who appear to be very different can turn out to be quite similar.

The most important principle for valuing diversity is *The Platinum Rule*. This is an expansion of The Golden Rule. The Golden Rule is a time-honored practice that is a foundation of many religious disciplines. In telling us to "treat others as you want to be treated," its intentions are sound. It was designed to prevent us from doing harm to others—things which others obviously would not like.

With the increasing complexity of our society, we now need to extend The Golden Rule because it does not account for people's different and unique needs. We cannot assume that others want to be treated exactly the way we do. By assuming that everyone else wants what we do, we perpetuate the values and beliefs of the dominant culture. The Platinum Rule gives others permission to be different from us, and reminds us to honor that difference.

The Platinum Rule is:

> "Treat others as they want to be treated."

Using The Platinum Rule makes it okay for us to have differences. In the classic 1973 *Harvard Business Review* article, "What It's Like to Be a Black Manager," Edward Jones notes that removing the "taboo" of discussing differences is the first step toward valuing them.

The "fine line" of discussing differences is that they should be *work related* and *behaviorally oriented*. People should not feel they are being judged or labeled because of their differences.

 • Why do you think The Platinum Rule may be more effective for valuing diversity than The Golden Rule?

• How do we find out how others want to be treated?

Managing Diversity
Versus Traditional Management

**Traditional
management**

Traditional management is defined as the effective and efficient utilization of employees in pursuit of the organization's goals and objectives.

Managing diversity

Managing diversity is defined as a comprehensive management process for creating an environment that enables *all* members of a workforce to be productive, without advantaging or disadvantaging *anyone*. (Thomas, *Harvard Business Review*, 1990)

Corning Glass, a pioneer in the area of diversity, views *courage* as one of the key requirements for successfully managing diversity—courage in questioning our own assumptions, overcoming old habits, making unpopular decisions, and extending beyond our comfort zones. A Corning brochure gives these examples:

> When a white employee is passed over for a new position, it is tempting—but dishonest—to smooth over disappointment by attributing a black colleague's promotion to race rather than talent. When filling a high level manufacturing position it's easy—but wrong—to assume that a woman would not be the best candidate because we are trapped by old stereotypes that women are not tough enough to lead in the plant environment. Leading diversity requires the courage to address such daily issues with openness and honesty.
>
> (Corning Glass brochure, 1990)

- How is managing diversity different from traditional management?

- What additional skills may be required for managing diversity?

- What are some reasons managers might resist managing diversity?

- What do managers have to gain by becoming good at managing diversity?

How Managers Set a Tone for Valuing Diversity

Setting the tone for an environment that values diversity is the *single most important* thing managers can do to encourage their people to value diversity. Managers need to do these three things to set the tone:

- Be a role model

- Use The Platinum Rule

- Project positive self-fulfilling prophecies

Be a role model

As their most basic foundation, managers must value diversity themselves and model the skills for valuing diversity. They must set their own behavior standards and live up to those standards. Being aware of people's individual differences and showing an appreciation for them are actions that team members will notice and begin to emulate.

Even more importantly, they must role model important decisions such as hiring, promotions, and rewards. Dr. R. Roosevelt Thomas described this common situation in a 1990 *Harvard Business Review* article.

When I asked a white male middle manager how promotions were handled in his company, he said, 'You need leadership capability, bottom-line results, the ability to work with people, and compassion.' Then he paused and smiled. 'That's what they say. But down the hall, there's a guy we call Captain Kickass. He's ruthless, mean-spirited, and he steps on people. That's the behavior they really value. Forget what they say.'

If behavior which is in direct opposition to valuing diversity is allowed to go uncorrected, people will get the real message that "this is just lip service." Managers must "walk the talk" for change to occur.

 • How else can managers be role models and "walk the talk"?

How Managers Set a Tone for Valuing Diversity, (continued)

Use the Platinum Rule

A principle of valuing diversity which is especially important for managers is The Platinum Rule: Treat others as *they* want to be treated.

People who attempt to manage diversity using The Golden Rule (treat others as *you* want to be treated) can unintentionally project their own backgrounds, perceptions, values, and beliefs onto others whose needs are dramatically different. For example, managers who value public recognition for themselves can unknowingly demotivate more reserved or modest employees by lavishing them with public praise.

Use of The Golden Rule also can lead to a "one size fits all" management approach. The "treat everyone the same" approach was popular in the 1970s as an effort to eliminate discriminatory treatment of nontraditional employees. Women tried to look like men ("Dress for Success"), minority employees hid their ethnicity, and managers attempted to treat everyone like a traditional white male employee. But people aren't all the same, and even all white males aren't the same. It is now widely accepted that this outdated approach is less effective than one in which managers tailor their styles for each employee. It is more important now than ever to be flexible; using one standard system that fits the manager will limit the productivity of the employees.

How can a manager learn the individual aspects of each employee? One way is through informal *interviews* with each person. (See the instrument, Manager/Employee Interview—Questions, page 266.) Managers who have abandoned the "one size fits all" approach ask these questions even in a homogeneous environment, because the answers can be so useful in determining what motivates each individual employee. The manager can provide people with a list of the questions to be discussed ahead of time, so people will have time to think about them. Most employees find this process to be rewarding, because it demonstrates that the manager cares about their unique needs and concerns. In addition, all these questions can be asked without crossing over the line of prying about someone's personal life, or violating employment law, because all questions are work related.

- What are some other ways managers can get to know their employees' unique needs?

How Managers Set a Tone for Valuing Diversity, (continued)

Project positive self-fulfilling prophecies

The "self-fulfilling prophecy" phenomenon is especially important for managers. In 1969, Harvard University conducted a study in which elementary school teachers were told that 205 of the students were "intellectual bloomers," but that they were not to treat them any different than the other students. In reality, the students were picked at random and had average IQs. At the end of the research, the "bloomers" showed gains of intelligence much higher than their classmates. (CRM Films, *The Pygmalion Effect*, 1989)

A similar study was conducted by Harvard at a vocational training center for the "hard-core unemployed." Foremen were told that five welders had high aptitude, while these men were actually chosen at random. At the end of the study, the selected welders were absent less than the control group, learned to weld in about half the time, and scored ten points higher on the welding test. Even more amazingly, fellow trainees selected these welders as "the people they most wanted to work with." The foremen said they had treated all the welders the same. (CRM, The *Pygmalion Effect,* 1989)

The implications of the self-fulfilling prophecy in the workplace are dramatic. Because of stereotypes we all have been raised with, we may be projecting onto others self-fulfilling prophecies that actually end up occurring. For example, traditional employees might be presumed to be competent, while others are presumed to be less competent until they prove otherwise. (Braham, "No, You Don't Manage Everyone the Same," *Industry Week*, 1989)

The manager's role in this dynamic process is critical because the manager is in a position authorized to extend or withhold rewards. If we assume people will fail, they often do—largely as a result of our expectations. The opposite is true as well. As managers, wouldn't we rather enter the situation with the assumption that people *are* competent and *will* succeed, until we see otherwise? The self-fulfilling prophecy is especially important with nontraditional employees because the traditional work environment has automatically viewed them as less competent, putting them at an immediate disadvantage.

- Has a manager of yours ever projected a positive or negative self-fulfilling prophecy onto you? What happened?

Diversity Employment Issues for Managers

Managers need to be aware of two critical employment issues and how they relate to diversity. These are:

- Staffing

- Performance management

Staffing

The most obvious sign that a company has begun to value diversity is when nontraditional employees are actively recruited, hired, and promoted into positions of authority. As we know from the *Workforce 2000* demographics, nontraditional employees form an increasingly large portion of new entrants to the workforce, which will rise to 85 percent of new entrants by the year 2000.

The goal of any recruiting, hiring, or promotion effort is to find the candidate who can best fulfill the responsibilities of the job. The purpose of interviewing, then, is to determine to what degree the applicant is capable of fulfilling the requirements of the job. The purpose is *not* to determine whether the person is *similar to* the person he or she is replacing, whether the person is *like us*, or whether we have anything in common with the person.

Recruiting is an area in which the structural blocks to valuing diversity become obvious. Often, well-intentioned managers report that they "couldn't find any nontraditional candidates" and that they "just aren't out there." What often happens is that recruiting sources (word of mouth, traditional recruiters and advertisers, etc.) do not reach or appeal to anyone but traditional candidates. The outcome is that only traditional candidates apply.

Another practice that occurs when trying to hire more diverse candidates is that the interview process screens people out based on old methods of interviewing and making decisions. "Gut feeling" and assumptions about "how well the person will fit in" are often the overriding issues. In a homogeneous workforce, it may seem like hiring someone who is different takes more effort; hiring this person may require different management practices, and stronger interpersonal skills from co-workers. These reasons, rather than the applicant's job competence, can often dominate the hiring decision.

To ensure that they are interviewing and evaluating the person based on competence, managers can use a method called *behavioral interviewing*. In behavioral interviewing, the focus is on what the person has done in the past—the person's *actions*, not on what the person *says* he or she would *like* to do. Because of this, hypothetical "what-if" questions are not the primary factor, nor is the person's skill at interviewing.

Diversity Employment Issues for Managers, (continued)

The assumption behind behavioral interviewing is that past behavior is the best predictor of future performance. By asking specific questions about what the person has done, the manager can form an accurate prediction of what the person will do in this job. This is not to imply that nonbehavioral questions should never be asked. The point is, the entire decision should not be based on subjective questions, which give no indication of what the person is likely to do. Behavioral interviewing also ensures that the focus is on the job, so illegal questions are not asked.

Behavioral questions

Examples of behavioral interviewing questions are:

- Please describe your present job duties and responsibilities.

- Describe a situation that demonstrates your greatest strength/ weakness.

- What in your background particularly qualifies you for this job?

- Describe a situation when you didn't handle something as well as you would have liked. What happened?

- What accomplishment are you most proud of?

- What do you like best/least about your present job?

- In the past, have you worked best independently or as part of a team? Describe a situation that demonstrates this.

- Is there anything that would prevent you from being able to travel 20 percent of the time?

Nonbehavioral questions

Examples of questions which are *not* behaviorally oriented are:

- Why do you like sales/accounting/purchasing, etc.?

- Describe your ideal job for me.

- What are your greatest strengths/weaknesses?

- What sports / hobbies do you enjoy?

Illegal questions

Examples of questions which are *illegal* are:

- Are you married or single?

- How old are you?

- Do you have children?

- Where are you from originally?

- Is your name Jewish/Italian/Chinese, etc.?

Diversity Employment Issues for Managers, (continued)

As human beings, it is natural for us to gravitate toward people who seem like us, and away from people who seem different. Think about the people you have hired and promoted, and your own elements of diversity. How similar to or different from you are the people you have hired and promoted in the past?

Performance management

Once an employee is hired, the manager's primary task becomes effective management and development of the person's performance. This consists of four basic steps, which are perfect opportunities to apply The Platinum Rule to management:

- Set and communicate performance expectations.
- Use appropriate motivational approaches.
- Provide meaningful feedback.
- Provide appropriate rewards and recognition.

Dr. Susan Resnick-West, co-author of *Designing Performance Appraisal Systems*, discovered in working with numerous organizations that "the only predictor of the success of a performance management system is whether it is customized for individuals." These management principles are just as effective with a homogeneous workforce as they are with a diverse one and have been accepted as most effective for many years.

Expectations

In the modern business environment, which requires high productivity to maintain profitability, goals are *essential*. The first step, setting and communicating specific performance expectations, is a critical business practice. If we don't know where we're going, how are we going to get there? The most effective method for setting expectations is for the manager and employee to do it together, based on input from the employee's internal and / or external customers.

When expectations are *not* set, it is usually for one of five reasons:

1. The manager and employee didn't think of it.
2. The manager and employee didn't have time.
3. The manager and employee didn't have enough information to set realistic ones.
4. The manager didn't want to get "locked in" to having to reward someone who succeeded.
5. The employee didn't want to get "locked in" to a specific performance standard (although, it is the manager's job to overcome this objection).

Diversity Employment Issues for Managers, (continued)

No one has the luxury of just hanging around, not contributing. It's easy to become so focused on "making the numbers" that we don't relate overall corporate goals to people's specific jobs. This leaves employees feeling unsure about what the highest priorities are, and how they will be evaluated for their contribution. In addition, nontraditional employees may not have as natural an understanding of the company's culture as traditional employees, so a lack of clear objectives has an even more detrimental effect on nontraditional employees.

Motivation

The second step of effective performance management—using appropriate motivational approaches—includes listening to the person's responses to the interview questions (see the assessment, Manager/Employee Interview—Questions, page 266) and following through with the approaches and rewards they value most. For employees who value independence, giving them freedom will be motivating. For employees who value lots of direction, giving them one-on-one time and guidance will be motivating. It all depends on the employee's particular preferences.

Feedback

Once performance expectations have been agreed upon, employees need *meaningful feedback* from their customers, peers, and manager on their progress toward these goals. This includes both positive and negative feedback. Contrary to popular belief, *employees want feedback*—even if it is not 100 percent positive. Most people would prefer knowing that they need to improve a few things than not know. Some people shy away from saying anything negative or from giving bad news, or they may think feedback will make no difference. In reality, avoiding giving a "weaker person" honest feedback deprives the person of improvement opportunities. Then the negative self-fulfilling prophecy begins, and the employee is labeled as "not competent" without having the opportunity to improve.

Rewards

Providing appropriate rewards and recognition is the positive side of feedback. In managing a diverse workforce, the rewards and recognition need to be what the *employee* wants—not what the manager is most accustomed to giving. Managers can simply ask employees what they prefer for a job well done, or can find innovative rewards from which the employee can select.

Diversity Employment Issues for Managers, (continued)

- Think of people you manage. How clear do you think they are on what is expected of them?

- Think of an employee—preferably one who is different from you—who recently had a performance problem. How did you handle it?

- What types of rewards do you usually offer people? How well do you think they match up with the person's individual preferences for rewards?

Notes

- _____
- _____
- _____
- _____
- _____
- _____
- _____
- _____
- _____
- _____
- _____
- _____
- _____
- _____
- _____
- _____
- _____
- _____
- _____
- _____
- _____

Team Guidelines and Communication for Managers

Two actions a manager can take to create an environment for valuing diversity are to establish team guidelines and communication processes which will support innovation, openness, flexibility, and teamwork.

Team guidelines

Managers can begin this effort by observing themselves and their team on the following characteristics of group dynamics:

- Who talks and who listens? (Look for air time, interruptions, withdrawal from participating.)

- Who is influential? (Whose ideas are utilized and whose are not, who agrees or disagrees with whom?)

- How are decisions made? (By vote, consensus, compromise, mandate?)

- How is conflict managed? ("Win lose," avoidance, "win win?")

- How is feedback managed? (Encouraged, stifled?)

Then, after analyzing these components, the manager can work with the group to establish four positive rules, or norms, required for effective group interaction. The manager needs to give special attention to any elements of group dynamics that might be obstacles. The four positive group norms are:

- Open membership (All members, including new and nontraditional ones, are accepted with equal privileges.)

- Shared influence (on goals, decisions, priorities)

- Mutual respect

- Candor (People can challenge each other, disclose openly.)

Communication

Managers also need to monitor their *own* communication processes with members of the team. The manager has an especially important role to play in communication, because he or she can demonstrate a value for all members by sharing information equally with everyone.

Informal social or communication networks exclude people from important opportunities to gain information. This is one of the structural issues which is often an obstacle to creating a workplace which values diversity. The people in the traditional network don't perceive any advantage associated with the network. However, if they think about information they have gained or relationships they have built as a result of their associations with these networks, or if they are asked to give these networks up, they often realize how important they have been. (e.g., the "golf group," after-hours parties, etc.).

Team Guidelines and Communication for Managers, (continued)

Other methods of informally sharing information can also exclude people. Because we tend to gravitate to people who are like us, we want to spend more time having lunch, doing projects, or even just chatting informally with them. Managers are in a position of special power and authority, and as such must share information with *everyone* who needs it, not just those with whom they are most comfortable.

- In reviewing the elements of group dynamics, which ones are the most effective in the group you manage?

- Which of the four positive group norms might need to be developed or modified?

- Think of a piece of important information of which you recently became aware. Did you share it with anyone? Is there anyone whom you *didn't* share it with, who could have benefited from knowing?

- What are some ways you could share information with people on your team with whom you normally don't have informal communication?

Chapter Seven:

Learning Activities

In this chapter of the sourcebook, you will find icebreakers / introductions, facilitated learning activities, and summary activities for use in your workshops. The activities are the foundation of people's active learning in the workshops, because it is during them that people come to their own "ah ha's" about diversity.

CHAPTER OVERVIEW

Each activity contains the following segments:

- Objective
- Time
- Materials
- Procedure
- Debrief
- Enhancement or alternative (for selected activities only)

How to Use the Activities

You can use the activities in a variety of ways:

- As part of the workshop guides provided
- As part of your own customized session
- To stimulate your thinking in creating your own activities

A few activities also include handouts to give to participants during the workshop. Note that diagrams of any prepared flipcharts can be found in the workshop guides in Chapters 3, 4, and 5.

You will find all of this chapter's activities in one or more of the workshop guide chapters. In those chapters they are part of a suggested design which effectively builds to a conclusion in which people are most likely to commit to valuing and managing diversity.

You can modify the guides or activities for your own needs, or use them as is. That's the beauty of *The ASTD Trainer's Sourcebook* — you can customize as much or as little as you like.

Workshop Guidelines

Objectives   The objective of this activity is to warm up participants and establish an environment in which they will feel comfortable with self-disclosure. Have the group establish its own ground rules for disagreement and encourage participants to regulate their own environment. Set a tone in which people know it is okay to share personal experiences (which is often not the norm in a business setting) and take charge of their own learning and environment.

Time
- 5 minutes

Materials
- Prepared flipchart, Workshop Guidelines (page 60) and marker.
- Noisemakers and fun items.

Procedure   Tell the group that diversity is a topic which deals with people's values and long-held beliefs. As such, people often disclose personal stories; sometimes there is also disagreement between people's views. Disagreement is okay, and is even encouraged—so long as people feel this is a safe environment where they won't be attacked or labeled personally. We don't want people sitting there disagreeing and not saying anything. One of the reasons for having diversity workshops is to give people a "laboratory" in which to test out their ideas with others. Tell people the workshop is *their* session and, as such, they make the rules. Ask them the following question:

- What do you need to feel comfortable opening up and disclosing today?

To get things going, say that sometimes groups list things like "Nothing we say leaves the room." Usually, people nod and ask that this be put on the list. Write this on the flipchart. Then ask:

- What else do you need?

Wait for a response; don't just move on. If people don't respond, say, "This is your list—is this all you need?"

Once a few items are on the list, if no one has addressed conflict, ask:

- If someone disagrees with you, how would you like them to do it?

Workshop Guidelines (continued)

Debrief Once the list is completed, post it on the wall. Tell people that because this is *their* list, they will enforce it. Hand out fun items such as noisemakers, whistles, koosh balls, etc. which people can use as signals that someone has violated a guideline. Summarize by saying that this light-hearted approach enables people to open up, and to give each other feedback in a nonthreatening way. It is also an indication that fun is allowed. Close by encouraging people to spontaneously have fun at any time.

Notes

- _____
- _____
- _____
- _____
- _____
- _____
- _____
- _____
- _____
- _____
- _____
- _____
- _____
- _____
- _____
- _____
- _____
- _____
- _____
- _____
- _____
- _____
- _____

On the Outside—
Icebreaker and Introductions

Objective

The purpose of this icebreaker is to help participants reconnect with how they felt to be on the outside at some point in their lives. This will enable them to have empathy for others who are on the outside in various situations in the workplace. It also creates a flip-chart list of the negative impact of excluding people, which can be used later in the workshop.

Time

- 20 minutes (25 minutes with enhancement)

Materials

- Prepared flipcharts, Introductions and "One Word" (pages 60 and 61, respectively) and marker

---

Procedure

Tell the group they are going to introduce themselves, first to a partner and then to the entire group. Their introductions should include the following points (which you can write on a flipchart):

- Name

- Department

- How long with the company

- How it felt to be on the outside

For the last point, ask them to tell their partners their stories of what happened and how it affected them. When they introduce themselves to the entire group, they will only give one word to summarize how they felt.

Demonstrate by introducing yourself. Include both your entire story and your one word.

Debrief

Ask participants to volunteer to introduce themselves and to share their one word. As they do, write their words on a flipchart. When everyone is finished, review the list. Discussion questions include:

- How would someone who was feeling these things behave at work?

- How would these feelings affect a person's productivity?

- What impact would it have on a team if a member felt this way?

Summarize by saying that we have all been on the outside at some time in our lives. By remembering how it felt, we can better empathize with co-workers who are different, or who represent an opinion that is different from that of the majority.

On the Outside—(continued)

Enhancement In addition to the suggested introduction points, add the following:

- A goal, hope, or concern for the workshop

  During their introductions, write participants' goals for the workshop on a flipchart next to the "One Word" flipchart. Tell people whether the goals are going to be addressed during the day or not. Use those that are going to be addressed to add emphasis to your comments during appropriate segments of the workshop to make it more meaningful. At the end of the session, have people review their original goals for a sense of accomplishment.

Alternative Or, add this question to the introduction:

- What is the biggest diversity issue in your department or team?

  Write the participants' diversity issues on a flipchart. Use the issues as case studies or examples throughout the session.

Notes
- _____
- _____
- _____
- _____
- _____
- _____
- _____
- _____
- _____
- _____
- _____
- _____
- _____
- _____
- _____
- _____
- _____
- _____
- _____

My Dimensions of Diversity— Icebreaker and Introductions

Objective

This activity enables people to get to know each other while gaining a deeper understanding of the Primary and Secondary Dimensions of Diversity. It helps people to realize that we differ on an infinite number of dimensions. It can be used with people who have never met, as well as with those who want to know each other at a deeper level.

Time

*   20 minutes

Materials

*   Handout, Primary and Secondary Dimensions of Diversity (page 173)
*   Blank flipchart
*   Blank stick-on name tags and pens

Procedure

Review the handout, Primary and Secondary Dimensions of Diversity. Ask people what they would add to the dimensions.

*   What are other aspects of how we're different, which make us who we are as people?

List responses on the blank flipchart.

Give everyone a name tag, and ask them to write some information about themselves on it, including:

*   Name
*   One primary dimension of diversity
*   One secondary dimension of diversity
*   One dimension of diversity added by the group

After people write down their information, they are to walk around, mixing with other participants and sharing their information as quickly as possible. After about 5 minutes, ask everyone to take their seats.

Debrief

Suggested debrief questions are:

*   How many different dimensions did you encounter in meeting people?
*   How did it feel to disclose information about yourself?
*   In what ways are we alike and different?
*   Are we all equally diverse, or are some of us more diverse than others?

My Dimensions of Diversity (continued)

Summarize by saying that diversity extends far beyond the obvious dimensions of race and gender. People are similar and different in an infinite number of ways. By viewing the idea of valuing diversity as something that is equally relevant to all of us, it becomes inclusive and liberating for everyone.

Notes

- _____
- _____
- _____
- _____
- _____
- _____
- _____
- _____
- _____
- _____
- _____
- _____
- _____
- _____
- _____
- _____
- _____
- _____
- _____
- _____
- _____
- _____
- _____
- _____

What's My Line?—
Icebreaker and Introductions

Objective

This activity illustrates the importance of first impressions and the impact of stereotyping, while getting to know people's names. Use this activity with people who do not know each other.

Time

• 20 minutes

Materials

• Overhead, Perceptions and Stereotypes (page 279)

Procedure

Tell people they are going to introduce the person to their right to the group. However, they will do this strictly by guesswork and assumptions. They can not talk to the person except to obtain their name.

After brief observation, they introduce the person by name. They state the person's job and favorite hobby, giving brief reasons for their guesses.

The person being introduced then responds with the correct information before proceeding with his or her introduction of the next person.

Debrief

Suggested questions are:

• How long does it take to form a first impression?

• How accurate are first impressions?

• What do we base them on?

• Have you ever opted not to interact with someone, based on a first impression?

Refer to the information on the overhead, Perceptions and Stereotypes.

Summarize by saying that first impressions are formed very quickly, within 30 seconds, and can be long-lasting. However, they are often inaccurate. In valuing diversity, we need to keep an open mind and transcend our stereotypes in order to give people the opportunity to let us discover who they really are.

Primary and Secondary Dimensions of Diversity

Objectives

This activity helps people to see the differences between primary and secondary dimensions of diversity. It helps participants understand that diversity applies to everyone because it includes much more than the obvious dimensions of race and gender.

Time

- 5 minutes

Materials

- Handout and overhead, Primary and Secondary Dimensions (pages 173 and 275, respectively).

Procedure

Say the following:

- In the 1991 book *Workforce America!*, authors Loden and Rosener define diversity in terms of two dimensions: primary and secondary. Primary dimensions are those that we are born with. People are usually the most sensitive about these dimensions because others can tell these things about us (with the exception of sexual preference) just by looking at us. So if someone has a preconceived idea about a certain dimension, they can project that onto someone before the person even opens his or her mouth.

- The secondary dimensions are those that we have some control over. These can change throughout our life. People also have a choice of whether they want to disclose this information or not. Because of this, people usually aren't as sensitive about these dimensions, even though these may have as big an impact on who we are as the primary dimensions.

Then, ask people to call out additional dimensions that contribute to who we are as people, (that aren't already listed on the chart). Write these around the outside as people call them out. (Examples might be family upbringing, personality style, political affiliation, lifestyle, hobbies, etc.) Comment and reinforce as people volunteer ideas.

Primary and Secondary
Dimensions of Diversity (continued)

Provide the following example:

- Personality type is an excellent example. How many people are familiar with the Myers-Briggs Type Indicator? It's an instrument that indicates our preference for one of 16 types. If you administered it to a group of 30-year-old white men and a group of 60-year-old Chinese women, both groups would split into the 16 types. You would find that a white man and a Chinese woman who had the same personality type actually *think* more like each other than the people who share demographic similarities.

Debrief

Ask the group:

- Who do you think the term *diversity* is referring to?

- Are we all equally diverse, or are some of us more diverse than others?

Summarize by saying that diversity extends far beyond the obvious dimensions of race and gender. People are similar and different on an infinite number of variables. By viewing the idea of "valuing diversity" as something that is equally relevant to all of us, it becomes inclusive as well as liberating for everyone.

Notes

- _____
- _____
- _____
- _____
- _____
- _____
- _____
- _____
- _____
- _____
- _____
- _____
- _____
- _____

Stepping Stones

Objectives   This activity helps participants reflect on the events and people which have most influenced their organization. The objective is to help people see which influences in their lives have the strongest bearing on who they are.

Time   • 30 minutes

Materials   • Small stones (or pieces of Play Doh)

Procedure   Ask people to answer this question individually to determine how the organization has evolved into what it has become:

• What series of six to eight stepping stones has led this organization to the diversity environment it has today?

Tell people that when they are finished they will each describe to their small group the stepping stones they identified. As they lay down a stone to symbolize each step, they will state their observations about it and how it affected them.

Debrief   Ask participants if anyone would care to share their observations on this activity. Ask them:

• What was more significant: things or people?

• How would your view of these events be different, if the time frame was five years prior to now or five years from now?

Summarize by saying that everyone has their own perception of the organization. All perceptions are accurate depending on whose eyes we are looking through. Reflecting on our organization can help us to understand the way things are today, and to determine key actions to help us create positive change in the future. Organizations are influenced by a variety of factors in their evolution, and understanding them gives us a wider perspective not only on the past, but on the future as well.

Alternative   Instead, have the stepping stones be personal. Tell participants that who we are is a result of many influences on us throughout our lives. Ask people to work individually to answer the following question:

• What series of six to eight stepping stones have led me to where I am in my life right now?

Stereotypes

Objective

The objective of this activity is to make explicit the prevalence of stereotypes in society and to help people realize we are all affected by them.

Time

- 25 minutes

Materials

- Handout and overhead, Stereotypes (pages 184 and 279, respectively)

- Ten prepared flipcharts

- Markers (all same color) for all participants

Procedure

Prepare ten flipcharts prior to the session, each with a primary or secondary dimension of diversity. Select these strategically, based on the composition of your group, so that they include many people in the room but exclude any highly volatile dimensions. For legal reasons, each flipchart should have the following words at the top: "Society's Stereotypes of" and at the bottom: "Do not use."

Society's Stereotypes of Accountants

(You will need ten flipcharts, each with a different element of diversity. Examples may include: Asians, Working Mothers, People with Military Background, Gays/Lesbians, People over 50, Catholics, Single People, MBAs, New Yorkers.)

Do Not Use

Stereotypes (continued)

 During a break, or before the session, post these around the room. Staple a blank sheet behind them so the markers don't bleed through to the wall as people write on them.

 Tell participants that generalizations are a necessary part of the way our brains function. We have so much data coming at us, that our brains can only pay attention to a small percentage of it. The rest is sorted by category so we don't have to think about it. Generalizations become negative when we filter out evidence which contradicts our preconceived ideas, and see only what we expected— what fits our stereotype.

 Ask people to take a marker and, as quickly as they can, go around the room and write a stereotype they have heard in society (*not* their own) on each flipchart. The only rule is that they can't repeat one that is already listed. They will have 5 to 10 minutes to do this.

Debrief   Usually, people begin joking and laughing as they write and read the stereotypes. When everyone has finished, read the charts, and returned to their seats, ask the following questions:

- How do you feel, seeing all these stereotypes?

- What percent are negative? Why are so many negative?

- Is anyone exempt from being stereotyped?

- How does it feel to know people may be stereotyping you in these ways?

- What impact does it have on a person, if we perceive that person according to what is on these flipcharts?

- Does anyone know of a person (other than yourself) who doesn't fit one of these stereotypes? When we do, is our tendency to change our stereotype, or to say "they're the exception?" (e.g., "He's not your typical New Yorker.")

- Do you think these stereotypes ever creep into this organization?

- What would happen to teamwork in this organization if we viewed people this way?

Stereotypes (continued)

You will need to facilitate the debrief with the clear goal of pulling the following observations from people.

- Stereotypes are pervasive in society. It took only about 5 minutes to come up with nearly X number (100, etc.).

- Even if we don't consciously think of them, they affect us.

- Most of the stereotypes are negative. We perceive the negative first and most often.

- We are all subject to negative stereotyping by others.

- We constantly make others prove us wrong in our negative assumptions, rather than assuming the best.

- When people don't fit the stereotype, we think they're the exception rather than questioning our stereotype.

- We need to heighten our awareness to keep stereotypes from influencing our perceptions of others as they really are.

 You can also choose topics for the flipcharts which are less volatile; for example, using professions only, or using society's stereotypes of men with earrings, etc. However, this greatly lessens the impact and the connection to the primary and secondary dimensions.

Addition At the end of the workshop, tell everyone to stand up for a ceremony (just like the kids at the end of the optional video, "A Class Divided"). Tell them to go to the flipchart of their choice, rip it off the wall, and tear it up, sharing if there are more people than flipcharts. Go around with a waste basket and collect the flipcharts. Summarize by saying that these stereotypes are not wanted in this organization. This is usually a very liberating and energizing activity, and quite symbolic. It can be made more fun through humor, "I want to hear *ripping*!" "Pick a chart you *really* disagree with!" etc.

Notes

- _____
- _____
- _____
- _____
- _____
- _____
- _____
- _____

Real-Life Goals

Objective

This activity gives participants an opportunity to obtain feedback on their behavior and create real-life goals to improve their own value for diversity. This is best used near the beginning of the session, in helping people focus on meaningful goals for the workshop, but it must be done after a warm-up or icebreaker.

Time

- 20 minutes

Materials

- Diversity Participant Developmental Needs—Feedback Request (page 217)

Procedure

Two to four weeks prior the workshop, send the Diversity Participant Developmental Needs—Feedback Request to four to six people who work with each workshop participant, asking them for anonymous feedback on the participant's behavior in valuing diversity. Also send the letter to the participants, asking them to answer the questions for themselves.

When the responses are returned (one to two weeks prior to the session), compile and summarize the results for each individual and put the results into individually sealed envelopes.

During the session, or one week prior to the session, give each person the sealed envelope with his or her feedback. Include a letter instructing each person to create a real-life goal to keep in mind during the workshop, and to use afterward in any development efforts or as part of their performance review process.

During the session, have participants work in pairs to discuss the following questions:

- How do you feel about the feedback you received?

- What strengths can you build on in valuing diversity?

- What are some ways you can enhance your behavior in valuing diversity?

Also ask the group, optionally:

- How do you feel about this?

- Would anyone like to share their goal with the group?

Real Life Goals (continued)

Debrief   People should not be forced to disclose their goals to the group, because they could be very personal. However, if people want to share, encourage them to do so.

To summarize, state that our view toward diversity is based on values we have accumulated over a lifetime. Our perceptions on this do not change easily or quickly; but by gaining feedback from others, seeking support, and being conscious of our own behavior we can make tremendous progress. Encourage people to stay in contact with their partners after the session to act as diversity "sounding boards."

Notes

- _____
- _____
- _____
- _____
- _____
- _____
- _____
- _____
- _____
- _____
- _____
- _____
- _____
- _____
- _____
- _____
- _____
- _____
- _____
- _____

Diversity Participant Developmental Needs—Feedback Request

_____ is going to be a participant
_{name}

in the Valuing Diversity workshop on _____.
_{date}

Because you work closely with this person, please answer the following questions and return this letter anonymously to

_____ by _____ .
_{name   date}

The person you work with will use your feedback, combined with the feedback of others, to develop a personalized goal in developing behaviors that value diversity. Thank you for your input!

1. How would you describe this person's behavior in valuing diversity?

2. What is this person's greatest strength in valuing diversity?

3. Why do you think so?

4. What is this person's top developmental need in valuing diversity?

5. Why do you think so?

217

Share Our Ideas

Objective

The objective of this activity is to cultivate a large number of ideas and encourage ongoing thinking on diversity between intermittent sessions.

Time

• 15 minutes

Materials

• Extra-large Post-it notes

• Pens

Procedure

Tell everyone, in advance, to bring at least one idea on valuing diversity to the workshop. For example, ideas could be about:

• Ways to respond to bias situations

• Methods for making people feel included

• Ways to give feedback, tips for open communication, etc.

Instruct participants to write these on extra-large Post-it notes, in large letters, as they enter the room.

At the beginning of the session, review and reinforce the ideas, leaving them posted. These can then be referred to throughout the session as practical ways to handle diversity situations.

Debrief

At the end of the session, ask people to review the posted ideas. Ask the following questions:

• How many people gained at least one useful new idea today?

• Do these spark any additional ideas in your mind?

Summarize by saying that, while it may seem like there are a limited number of solutions to diversity issues, there are actually a large number of ways to handle them. By brainstorming, being creative, and applying ideas in new ways we can find many innovative ways to value diversity.

Notes

• _____

• _____

• _____

• _____

• _____

• _____

• _____

• _____

Bests and Worsts

Objective
This activity introduces the topic of diversity and stimulates people's thinking in a high-energy manner. This can also be used as a session-starter in multi-day or multi-week training to review the previous sessions ideas.

Time
- 20 minutes

Materials
- Two flipcharts, one labeled "Best" and one labeled "Worst"

- Markers

Procedure
Ask participants to call out the best and worst examples they can think of in diversity practices. As people call out their ideas, ask them to share their reasons for placing the items on the list. Write the best practices on one flipchart and the worst practices on another.

Then, have participants work quickly in small groups to do the following:

- Create five "do's" based on the "best" list.

- Create five "don'ts" based on the "worst" list.

You may ask participants to write their lists on flipchart paper. (This takes an additional 5 minutes.)

Debrief
Have each group report back with their lists. Comment on and reinforce their ideas. Summarize by saying that, often, valuing diversity is a matter of common sense, and it is easy to see practices which value diversity and those which do not. The key is being able to consistently act on this common sense.

Notes
- _____
- _____
- _____
- _____
- _____
- _____
- _____
- _____
- _____
- _____

Learning About Each Other

Objective

The objectives of this activity are to give participants an experience using The Platinum Rule, to provide people with a simple process for working through difficult issues individually or as a group, and to help participants learn more about a group which is different from them.

Time

- 45 to 60 minutes

Materials

- Prepared flipchart, Learning About Each Other (page 62)

- Two blank flipcharts and markers

Procedure

Divide the group into two, based on a primary dimension of diversity (either gender, age, or race). Tell them that they will go through a process which they can use to implement The Platinum Rule and to address difficult issues. The groups will go into separate rooms, and will have 15 to 20 minutes to brainstorm the top three answers to the following questions listed on the prepared flipchart:

- What problems do you experience in the workplace in relation to the other group?

- What can the other group do differently to improve the situation?

- What is your group willing to do to help them?

Each group needs to write their answers on a blank flipchart page for presentation to the other group.

Debrief

Once the groups have returned to the room, have one group present their answers to the other. The trainer should become "invisible" in this process, encouraging direct dialog between the groups. The trainer's role is to encourage increasing levels of openness between groups, and to redirect any attacks.

After the first group answers the first question, ask the other group, "How do you feel about their issues? Are they clear? Do you have any questions or reactions?" After the first group answers the second question, ask the other group, "Do you understand these? Do you think you can do them?" When the first group is finished, lead a round of applause for them. Go through the same process for the second group.

Learning About Each Other (continued)

Ask the groups:

- How did you feel going through this?

- How did the process of finding common ground help bring the groups together?

- What similarities were there between the groups' answers?

- Was this a useful process? How could you see it being used?

Summarize by saying that this process is useful for both individual and group interactions. Often, we do step one and forget steps two and three. By suggesting alternatives and taking responsibility for a positive outcome, we learn to work together to create a more productive environment.

Notes

- _____
- _____
- _____
- _____
- _____
- _____
- _____
- _____
- _____
- _____
- _____
- _____
- _____
- _____
- _____
- _____
- _____
- _____
- _____
- _____
- _____

Excluding Others

Objective

This activity provides participants with an experience that demonstrates how it feels to exclude others, as well as the experience of being excluded by others.

To help people identify ways to consciously include others

Time

- 25 minutes (35 minutes with expansion)

Materials

- None

Procedure

Divide participants into groups of 5 to 6 people. Ask for one volunteer from each group. Ask the volunteers to leave the room.

Explain to the remaining participants that each group is a work team. The person outside is a new member. Say that it is *common knowledge* (be sure to use these words) that the person was only hired because he or she knew the president. Everyone has *heard* this person is not qualified, and it is likely that the rest of the team is going to have to compensate for the person's lack of skills by working harder and putting in more hours. This is the person's first day. The group is going to have a meeting in which they plan their annual party.

Go outside and tell the volunteers that they are new employees, and that they are going to attend a meeting with their new work teams to plan the annual party. Tell the volunteers that they were hired after extensive interviews and that they are well qualified, having worked in a similar job for five years. Tell them that they were thrilled to be offered the job and are eager to get to work, although it is always awkward starting in a new organization where you don't know anyone. Bring them back into the room, and allow five to ten minutes for the team meeting. When finished, ask people to return to their original seats.

Debrief

Ask the excluded volunteers the following questions:

- How did the group treat you? Did they exclude you?

- How did it feel to be pre-judged, and not know why?

- What techniques did you use to try to overcome any exclusion? What does this tell you about yourself?

- What verbal and nonverbal messages did the group use to exclude you?

Excluding Others (continued)

[?] Ask the group members:

- To what degree did you exclude the volunteer?

- •Did anyone attempt to find out the volunteer's "story"?

- How far did you take your excluding behavior?

- What does this tell you about yourself?

[?] Ask the entire group:

- Does this happen in the workplace?

- How important is the "grapevine" and/or preconceived ideas, and their impact on our behavior?

- What impact do they have on our productivity? On teamwork?

Depending on the composition of the group, it may be beneficial to choose traditional employees as volunteers, and nontraditional employees as group members. This role reversal is sometimes enlightening for both.

Summarize by saying that we can often exclude people unconsciously; but this behavior is harmful to workplace productivity. Encourage people to consciously try to exhibit behaviors that include others, and to give people an opportunity before letting their preconceived ideas take over.

Expansion In small groups, have people brainstorm ways to consciously include others. When finished, have each group report back to the larger group. (This adds 10 minutes.)

Notes

- _____
- _____
- _____
- _____
- _____
- _____
- _____
- _____
- _____
- _____

Giving Feedback

Objectives

The objectives of this activity are to give participants criteria for giving other people feedback and to help participants feel more comfortable acting as change agents to create an environment which values diversity.

Time

- 30 minutes

Materials

- Effective Feedback Criteria (page 225)
- Giving Feedback—Case Studies (page 226)
- Blank flipchart

Procedure

Tell participants that an important element in creating an environment that values diversity is our ability to give people honest and open feedback without attacking them. Ask participants the following questions, writing their answers to questions 3, 4, and 5 on a flipchart:

1. Why do we avoid giving people feedback?

2. How do we feel about receiving feedback?

3. If someone objected to something you did, how would you want him or her to let you know?

4. What are some things you would *not* want him or her to do?

5. What would make it easier for us to give feedback?

Give each participant the handouts, Giving Feedback—Handout and Giving Feedback—Case Studies. Relate the criteria to their answers to the previous questions. Ask them to work in groups, pairs, or triads to answer the question at the bottom of the Giving Feedback—Case Studies sheet.

Debrief

Have each group share their answers to the questions. Ask the other groups to comment on and add to their solutions. Reinforce the groups' responses that correctly used the feedback criteria. Summarize by saying that these criteria help us to give feedback in a constructive way that informs but does not attack the other person. This can help us to be more proactive as change agents.

To determine what behavior is appropriate in the workplace ask this question: Does it positively contribute to the productivity of the team and the organization? If not, address it with the individual involved, or with the team if appropriate.

Effective Feedback Criteria

The following criteria for giving constructive feedback provides a straightforward way to let others know how their behavior negatively affects us.

☑ **Describe specific behavior**

Effective feedback describes observable *actions*, rather than assigning meaning to activities. It is descriptive, not judgmental.

☑ **Express feelings**

Good feedback tells someone how you *feel* about what he or she did. It is okay to say you are mad, frustrated, confused, or upset— so long as you direct your feelings toward the *behavior*, not the person.

☑ **Request alternatives**

Good feedback is proactive in asking for an alternative behavior, rather than just "dumping" the negative. State what you would like the person to do instead.

☑ **Consider everyone's needs**

Give effective feedback with the needs and feelings of both the sender *and* the receiver in mind.

☑ **Time it well**

Choose the time and situation for the feedback strategically. Try to do it as soon as possible after the incident. However, don't do it in the heat of the moment unless you can maintain your composure. Also, avoid a public discussion unless it is an issue for the entire team to address.

Example

After the meeting you say, (**timing**)

"Pat, remember that joke you made in the meeting today?" (**describe behavior**)

"Well, I feel uncomfortable laughing at someone else's expense." (**express feelings**)

"Maybe you could tell jokes which are neutral, and don't cut anyone down." (**request alternatives**)

"I really like your sense of humor, and I'd like your jokes a lot more if they were upbeat." (**consider everyone's needs**)

Giving Feedback—Case Studies

Case 1

> You are waiting for a team meeting to start. Five people are already there, and you are waiting for three more. A colleague is telling you that she is considering buying a new home. She describes a neighborhood which she is considering moving to, but she says she is uncertain because a lot of "those type of people" (a certain ethnic group) have recently moved into the neighborhood and she thinks it is "going bad."

Case 2

> You are at the coffee machine with three other people. Some-one mentions that the new person is starting today. Your co-worker says, "I heard she only got this job because she slept with you-know-who." He goes on to say that he believes it, because she's so pretty it's hard to believe she also has the brains to do the job.

Case 3

> You are walking down the hall with several co-workers, on the way back from a meeting. An employee from another depart-ment walks past you. One of the people says, "I heard he was gay. I don't mind gay people, but someone told me they saw him going into the bathroom with another gay guy, and they were in there a long time. I can tell you, I'll never go into the bathroom when they're in there."

- Why might the diversity violator say what he or she said?

- Using the feedback criteria, what exact words would you say to the person, and when and where would you give the feedback?

Appreciating Each Other

Objective

This activity helps people express appreciation and give feedback to each other. It works well with intact work groups or teams to build openness and appreciation between teammates.

Time
Materials

- 20 minutes
- Blank flipchart
- Name tags or tents
- Index cards
- Envelopes
- Pencils

Procedure

At a break prior to the end of the session, or at the end of a previous diversity session with this group, provide each person with a number of blank index cards equal to the total number of participants. (Note: If participants are not an intact work team, they must have name tags/tents so everyone knows each other's name.) Ask them to write each person's name on top of one card, and then to think about each person's behavior during the session. Write the following question on the flipchart and have the participants write their answers on each card.

- What is one thing the person did which I appreciated?

  Remind people to focus on behavior, not on their assumptions about each other. Also, tell people that we often focus on the negative in others; but by focusing on and communicating the positive, we help to create an environment that values diversity.

  Collect the cards, sort them, and put them in an envelope for each person (either on a break, or between sessions).

  Hand out the envelopes to each person (either at the end of the session, or during this activity at the next session). Have them scan the cards, think about them, and get into pairs to discuss:

  - How they feel about the feedback
  - Any comments that stand out to them

Debrief

Ask the participants if anyone would like to share the card which made them feel the best, or a card which was surprising or confusing.

Conclude by stating that we all have many positive attributes, and that having them acknowledged makes us feel appreciated and included—a key requirement for an environment of valuing diversity. Encourage people to give positive feedback to others they work with on a more frequent basis.

Appreciating Each Other (continued)

Expansion   Have people also answer the following question about each other:

 • What one thing do I think would help the person to grow?

Debrief   Debrief with the same questions. Summarize by adding that we often avoid giving feedback, which is a major obstacle to valuing diversity. By expressing our observations honestly and in a caring manner, and by being open to receiving feedback ourselves, we are able to bridge many differences and even help each other to grow.

Notes

• _____

• _____

• _____

• _____

• _____

• _____

• _____

• _____

• _____

• _____

• _____

• _____

• _____

• _____

• _____

• _____

• _____

• _____

• _____

• _____

• _____

• _____

Constructive Conflict

Objectives

The objectives of this activity are to provide people with a method for constructively handling conflict (which often goes unaddressed in diversity situations) and to help people become more aware of their own conflict style and strategies.

Time

- 30 minutes

Materials

- Constructive Conflict—Handout (page 231)

- Handout, Constructive Conflict—Case Studies (page 232)

- Blank flipchart

Procedure

Tell the group that conflict sometimes arises around diversity issues; but more often, we avoid conflict issues. They go unaddressed, but remain a sore spot which affects people's teamwork and productivity. Ask participants:

1. Why do people avoid conflict?

2. What are the sources of conflict?

3. What are the positive aspects of conflict?

4. What would make it easier to address conflict?

5. How would you want someone to address a conflict with you?

6. How can we demonstrate that we value someone, even though we have a conflict with them?

7. How do we usually respond when someone has a conflict with us and approaches us about it?

8. How could we make it easier for the person who initiates a conflict discussion with us?

Chart the responses to questions 5, 6, 7, and 8 on a flipchart.

Give participants the handouts, Constructive Conflict—Handout and Constructive Conflict—Case Studies. Tell them that everyone has a conflict style, that affects how they behave in conflict situations. Give them a minute to read the handouts.

Constructive Conflict (continued)

 Divide people into triads. Assign a case study to each triad, and tell them to spend 5 minutes role playing the case studies with the third person acting as an observer. Tell them to take a minute to prepare, remembering the ideas on the flipchart and handout. Tell the observer to look for ways in which the role players followed the flipchart and handout guidelines. The observer may want to take notes during the role play. The observer also needs to determine the conflict style each person used. When the role play is finished, the observer will give feedback to the role players and the triad will spend 5 minutes discussing what happened. The observer will report back to the larger group.

Debrief Have the observers report back to the group, with the other triads commenting on and adding to their solutions and analysis. Summarize by saying that we need to be proactive in addressing conflict, always remembering to use a cooperative, "win win" style.

Notes

- _____
- _____
- _____
- _____
- _____
- _____
- _____
- _____
- _____
- _____
- _____
- _____
- _____
- _____
- _____
- _____
- _____
- _____

Constructive Conflict—Handout

CONSTRUCTIVE CONFLICT GUIDELINES

Following are some ways to constructively resolve conflict:

- Agree upon a common goal of resolving the conflict so everyone wins—look for common ground.
- Demonstrate respect for the other person.
- Be open with your thoughts and feelings.
- Don't attack or blame the other person.
- Listen to the other person with an open mind.
- Value differences in viewpoint.
- Identify and understand your own and others' conflict styles.

Conflict Styles

Everyone has a conflict style. Understanding our own and others' styles is helpful in understanding and resolving conflict.

Avoidance

The *Avoider* would rather not address conflict at all, and is most comfortable ignoring or delaying issues and repressing his or her own feelings and needs. This is a "lose lose" style, because the conflict goes unaddressed and teamwork and productivity are usually negatively affected.

Competition

The *Competitor* tries to win the conflict at all costs, usually at the expense of the other person. This is a "win lose" style, in which one person may get what he or she wants, while the other person loses. While this style produces short-term victories, in the end it damages productivity because it hurts people's relationships.

Adaptation

The *Adaptor* is most comfortable giving in to the other person's needs, sacrificing his or her own goals. This is a "lose win" style, which appears cooperative but can be detrimental in the long run because it does not produce a win for all parties.

Cooperation

The *Cooperator* tries to find a solution that meets everyone's needs. In cooperation, the issues are fully explored, everyone states their needs, and people work together to find creative solutions in which everyone benefits. This is a "win win" style.

Constructive Conflict—Case Studies

Case 1

WHO STAYS AND WHO GOES?

Pat and Joe work on the same team. It's been a long day. It's almost quitting time, but work still needs to be done to make the big deadline tomorrow. One person is going to have to work late. Joe needs to leave right on time because of daycare issues. Joe has no one else who can pick up the baby. Pat doesn't have a specific commitment, but has worked late the last three nights. How do they resolve the conflict of who stays and who goes?

Case 2

WHAT'S SO FUNNY?

Terry and Chris work on the same team, but don't socialize much during breaks or lunch time. Terry hangs out with the Spanish-speaking group and Chris is part of the group who speaks Tagalog. Terry has been getting really irritated because every day at lunch, as Terry goes past Chris's group, it seems like they all laugh and then talk very fast in Tagalog. Terry mentioned it once to Chris, but Chris said that they weren't talking about Terry at all, that it was just Terry's imagination. In fact, Chris said the same thing about Terry's group—that they all laughed and talked very loudly in Spanish when Chris passed them at the water cooler once. Today was the last straw. Chris's group burst into laughter just as Terry walked in the lunch room. Terry has to say something to Chris.

Case 3

BRIDGING THE GAP

Carol and Jean usually work well together, even though there is a 40-year difference in their ages. One day, Carol brings in an article about Generation X and starts going on and on about how selfish "these youngsters" are and how they want to "have it all without paying the price." Jean starts to get upset, and says that when people get old, they start to get set in their ways—all you ever hear about is "the good old days" and how the world is "going to pot" with these younger generations. The conversation escalates into a full-fledged conflict. How do they resolve it?

Constructive Conflict—Case Studies (continued)

Case 4

PROFESSIONAL COURTESY

Bobby and Jan are both part of the team that provides service to their customer, Ajax. Bobby is in sales and Jan is in technical services. They are both very dedicated to serving the customer, but Bobby feels the customer relationship is most important while Jan thinks product excellence is more important. In a meeting last week, Jan said that it was fine and dandy that Bobby "spent all his time shmoozing," while Jan "worked like a dog" making sure they had a quality product. Bobby responded that all the "technical types" should just "stay in their little corner, away from my customers" because they "might scare them away" with their poor interpersonal skills. Now, when Bobby has to call and ask Jan for help with Ajax, Jan says, "I thought you wanted me to stay away from your customers!" How do they resolve this conflict?

Notes

- _____
- _____
- _____
- _____
- _____
- _____
- _____
- _____
- _____
- _____
- _____
- _____
- _____
- _____
- _____
- _____
- _____

Managing Diversity Versus Traditional Management

Objective

This activity helps participants understand how managing diversity may differ from our traditional view of management.

Time

- 15 minutes

Materials

- Handout, Managing Diversity Versus Traditional Management (page 189)

Procedure

Refer managers to the Managing Diversity Versus Traditional Management handout. Ask them to work in their small groups to answer the questions on the handout, which are:

- How is managing diversity different from traditional management?

- What additional skills may be required for managing diversity?

- What are some reasons managers might resist managing diversity?

- What do managers have to gain by becoming good at managing diversity?

Debrief

Have each group share their answers to the questions. Summarize by reinforcing the groups' responses. You might say that managing diversity is focused on the process of creating an environment in which everyone can be equally productive. Several skills are required, including valuing diversity, understanding our own perceptions and biases, relating to people as individuals, and being a champion of change. Courage is also a major requirement, as noted in the Corning Glass example. Managers might resist managing diversity because it takes time and effort, and it may be uncomfortable to learn at first. But the managers who will be in demand in the future are those who are good at managing a variety of people, not just people like themselves.

Notes

- _____
- _____
- _____
- _____
- _____
- _____
- _____

Key Factors for Managing Diversity

Objectives

The objectives of this activity are to help participants identify the key factors for managers in creating an environment which values diversity and to understand how their role as managers extends beyond that of a regular employee.

Time

- 20 minutes

Materials

- Prepared flipchart, Key Factors for Managing Diversity (page 63) and marker

- 3-foot by 5-foot piece of construction paper

- Repositionable mounting spray

- 8 1/2-inch by 5 1/2-inch colored paper

Procedure

Before the session, attach the construction paper to the wall. Cover it with the spray. Prepare two 8 1/2-inch by 5 1/2-inch colored sheets in large, bold print. One says *3 to 5 words* and the other says *big, bold letters*. Stick these to the construction paper.

Tell participants that they are going to use a process to define the key factors for effectively managing diversity. Explain that managers have a role beyond that of regular employees, because they are in positions which have the authority to influence the organization's infrastructures, such as hiring, promotions, pay increases, social norms, etc.

Hand out one 8 1/2-inch by 5 1/2-inch sheet to each person, with a stack in the middle of the table. Ask participants to work on their own and list at least five or six answers to the following question, which is written on the flipchart:

- What managerial behaviors will create an environment and infrastructures that value diversity?

After about 3 minutes, ask them to choose their top three ideas. Then ask them to work in small groups to share each person's top three ideas and choose the best three to four from the entire group. Refer to the construction paper, and tell them to summarize their ideas in three to five words, and write them on the colored sheets in big bold letters. When they are finished, ask them to stick their ideas to the paper.

Key Factors for Managing Diversity (continued)

Next, ask participants if any items can be grouped into pairs which are similar. For example, "Role Modeling" and "Setting a Good Example." Let participants guide this—all you do is move the papers as they direct. If a dispute occurs, the person who had the original idea has the final call. Continue until all possible pairs are formed. Ask people to name each pair, for example, "Role Modeling." Have someone write these, and number each pair (i.e., "1—Role Modeling," etc.).

Now, ask participants to review their original lists. Participants should summarize in three to five words any items that are not already posted, and write them on a sheet in big, bold letters. If people want to assign a group number to their idea, they should write this on the sheet. Collect and post the sheets, leaving unnumbered ones randomly posted.

Have people direct you in grouping the rest of the ideas until several columns are formed. This may require reviewing and adjusting the original lists.

Once all items have been placed, ask participants to review all the information and determine meaningful names for the lists. As people call out names, test these off of the group until one fits for everyone. Have someone write these on new sheets and post them.

Debrief

Tell participants that they now have a concise list of the (five or six) most important factors for them to act on in managing diversity. They may want to write these down, or create goals for themselves in these areas as a follow-up.

Enhancement

This activity can be linked to the Derailment Case Study for Managers on page 240. The key factors can be used as a guide for groups in analyzing the case study and formulating a solution. In the debrief after the case study, you can also ask people:

• What would you add to the "key factors" chart based on what you discovered in the case study?

• Is anything missing, or is it complete?

• How useful were these factors in analyzing the situation?

Real-Life Case Studies—Summary

Objective

This activity gives participants an opportunity to practice addressing diversity situations by finding solutions to their own real-life case studies. It is best used near the end of the session as a summary activity, after other diversity ideas, models, and practices have been discussed.

Time

- 20 minutes

Materials

- Handout/Letter, Diversity Case Study Preparation (page 238)

Procedure

Two to four weeks prior to the workshop, send the Diversity Case Study Preparation letter to participants asking them to think of a real-life situation involving diversity that they would like the group to address. When the responses are returned (one week prior to the session), go through them and select several for use in the workshop. Type and copy them for handouts.

In the session, ask participants to work in pairs or triads to create solutions to the case studies based on what they have learned during the day on diversity. Ask participants to answer the following questions:

- What are the top two or three issues in this case study?

- How would you address this situation, using what you have learned in this workshop?

Enhancement

This activity can be combined with other models in this sourcebook, such as Giving Feedback (page 224) or Constructive Conflict (page 229), to bring real-life case studies into the activity.)

Debrief

Have participants from each group read their case studies, and tell the group their answers. Have the rest of the participants comment and add to each group's solution.

Notes

- _____
- _____
- _____
- _____
- _____
- _____
- _____
- _____

Diversity Case Study Preparation

You are going to participate in the Valuing Diversity workshop on

_____. To make sure we give you a chance to
<u>date</u>

address real-life issues in the workshop, we ask that you give us a

case study regarding diversity which has happened to you, or which

you have heard about from others.

Please answer the question below and return this letter anony-

mously to _____ by _____.
<u>name</u>   <u>date</u>

Thank you for your input!

? Will you please describe a diversity incident that happened to you,
that you witnessed or heard about (recently if possible) that you
would like to see addressed in the workshop?

- _____
- _____
- _____
- _____
- _____
- _____
- _____
- _____
- _____
- _____
- _____
- _____
- _____
- _____

Derailment Case Study for Managers— Summary

Objective	This activity gives managers an opportunity to bring together their learning on managing diversity through a common case study. It is best used near the end of the session as a summary activity, after other ideas on managing diversity have been discussed.
Time	• 20 minutes
Materials	• Handout, Derailment Case Study for Managers—Handout (page 240)

Procedure

Ask participants to work in pairs or triads to create solutions to the case study based on what they have learned during the day on diversity. Ask participants to answer the following questions:

• What happened? What mistakes were made?

• How would you address this situation, using what you have learned in this workshop?

Debrief

Ask participants from each group to share their answers. Have the rest of the participants comment and add to each group's solution. Ask participants:

• Do you think this could happen in real life?

• Summarize by stating that managing diversity takes not only commitment, but advance preparation, planning, involvement of other team members, and ongoing communication and feedback.

Notes

• _____

• _____

• _____

• _____

• _____

• _____

• _____

• _____

• _____

• _____

• _____

Derailment Case Study for Managers—Handout

> ## CASE STUDY
>
> Six months ago, you took a big step in filling a job with a non-traditional employee. Previously, only traditional employees have held this job. It was a tough decision, and some people criticized you for it. Explaining to other traditional employees why they didn't get the job was tough, too. But you took the risk because Employee X had the skills, abilities, and experience needed to do the job. You were proud of your effort to go beyond the old stereotype of the job, and you felt good about Employee X's chances for success.
>
> Now, six months later, things seem to be going wrong. Employee X seems to be struggling. Employee X doesn't know things a person in that position should know by now. It seems like things are taking too long to get done. On top of this, Employee X's peers are complaining, "We knew Employee X wouldn't work out. This person just can't cut it here. Why not send Employee X to department Y? That type does a lot better over there."
>
> Employee X has come to you as well. "Why wasn't I invited to the planning meeting." Well, you thought it was too soon—you didn't want to overwhelm Employee X. "Why didn't I get a copy of the V.P.'s memo?" You just forgot—a natural mistake. "I feel like I don't know what I'm supposed to be doing." You gave Employee X a copy of the annual plan—why can't Employee X figure it out? You did notice a strange expression on Employee X's face when the gang was talking about the big outing last week. Why wasn't Employee X there?
>
> You aren't sure why, but it's obvious that Employee X is becoming derailed.

- What happened? What mistakes were made?

- What are you going to do?

A Vision of Valuing Diversity—Summary

Objective   This activity helps people use their creativity to imagine a workplace which truly values diversity, and to create action steps in achieving this vision.

Time   • 20 minutes

Materials   • Blank flipcharts (one chart or page for each group)

          • Multi-colored markers

Procedure   Divide the group into teams of four to six people each, at their tables if possible. Ask them to do the following:

1. Brainstorm as a group what this organization would be like if they had an environment which truly valued diversity.

2. Create a graphic image of their vision and draw it on their flipchart, using multi-colored markers. (They may want to conceal their image from the other groups for a grand "unveiling.")

3. Create two to three action steps which they, *as individuals*, can implement that will contribute to achieving this vision.

Debrief   Have each group present their vision and graphic image to the whole group. Then, have them list their action steps. The other groups can ask questions or make comments.

          Summarize by stating that we all want to work in an environment where we are free to be who we are, and to be appreciated for our unique contribution. Only by working together, as a team with a common goal, and following through with action can we create an environment that truly values diversity.

Notes   • _____

          • _____

          • _____

          • _____

          • _____

          • _____

          • _____

          • _____

          • _____

Changes in Viewpoint on Diversity— Summary

Objective   This activity gives participants an opportunity to review their learnings and to summarize their new views on diversity.

Time   • 5 minutes

Materials   • Overhead, Changes in Viewpoint on Diversity (page 283)

Procedure   Ask participants to reflect for a moment on their views about diversity prior to the session. Then, have them think about how they view diversity now.

Display the overhead, stating that these are some comments from other groups.

Debrief   Ask the following questions:

• How has your view of diversity changed since the beginning of this workshop?

• What are your key learnings?

• What is your biggest "take away"?

     Summarize by saying that diversity has progressed dramatically over the years, and that we need to continually remember these important points to be prepared for the workplace of the year 2000.

Notes   • _____

• _____

• _____

• _____

• _____

• _____

• _____

• _____

• _____

• _____

• _____

• _____

• _____

Chapter Eight

Instruments and Assessments

In this section of the sourcebook, you will find instruments and assessments for use during your workshops. These are a key piece of your trainer's tool kit because they allow people to determine where they stand in regard to diversity. They can be an important vehicle for people's self-discovery. They can also guide your organization into realizations about additional processes—besides training—which need to be addressed for a successful diversity effort.

HOW TO USE THE INSTRUMENTS AND ASSESSMENTS

You can use them in a variety of ways:

- To assess your organization's current position on diversity

- To stimulate participants' thinking and self-reflection before the workshop

- As 360-degree feedback for participants in the workshop

- As activities for participants during the workshop

- As lead-ins to other activities in the workshop

Organizational Climate Survey

Purpose   The purpose of this survey is to determine an organization's strengths, as well as obstacles to overcome, in creating an environment which values diversity.

Time
- 5 minutes to fill out survey
  5 minutes for discussion of results

Materials
- Handout, Organizational Climate Survey (page 245) and pencils

Procedure   Prior to beginning the diversity effort or during the workshop, have people complete the survey. Compile the results, and use them to determine the organization's greatest strengths to build upon for a successful diversity effort, as well as the obstacles that could get in the way and that need to be overcome. Compare results for different demographic groups to determine their different perceptions of the organization.

The results can also be used as an original benchmark before the workshops begin, and the survey can be readministered later (six months, one year, three years) to see what progress has been made.

The results can also be incorporated into memos or announcements and discussed during workshops, to help participants understand the strengths in the organization's current climate as well as the steps which are being taken to address obstacles. In particular, they should be incorporated into the Our Organization's Value for Diversity handout on page 169. In presenting the results in the workshop, it should be made clear that these are people's *perceptions* and are not necessarily statements of fact. However, perceptions are very important, and the organization is paying close attention to them.

Debrief   Ask participants the following questions:

- What do you think of these results?

- Do you think the results are accurate?

- What will the organization need to do to overcome these obstacles?

- How can we build on the organization's strengths?

       Conclude by saying that the organization is demonstrating a strong commitment by asking for employees' input and being open in sharing the results. Only through open communication and constant re-assessment of our progress will we create an environment which truly values diversity.

Organizational Climate Survey—Worksheet

Please answer the questions honestly and candidly. Your responses are *strictly* confidential, and will be compiled along with responses from many other employees. Do not put your name on this paper—it is anonymous.

Demographics: Check the boxes below that apply to you.

Race: ☒ Caucasian   ☐ African-American   ☐ Asian   ☐ Hispanic   ☐ Native-American

Gender: ☐ Male   ☒ Female

Age: ☐ under 30   ☒ 31 to 40   ☐ 41 to 50   ☐ 51 to 60   ☐ over 60

Have children? ☐ yes   ☒ no

Education: Check the boxes below that apply to you.

☐ did not complete high school   ☐ high school diploma   ☐ some college/vocational/technical

☐ associate's degree   ☒ bachelor's degree   ☐ master's degree   ☐ doctorate

Have been with the organization:

☐ less than 1   ☒ 1 to 5 years   ☐ 6 to 10 years   ☐ 10 to 20 years   ☐ more than 20 years

Position is: ☐ management   ☒ nonmanagement

Have been given a promotion (increase in responsibility and pay) here?   ☒ yes   ☒ no

---

Questions: For each question, circle the number that applies to you.

1. **How fulfilled are you in your job?**

   Not fulfilled   Moderately fulfilled   Very fulfilled
   1   2   ③   4   5   6   7   8   9   10

2. **How important is it to follow "unwritten rules" to get ahead here?**

   Not important   Moderately important   Very important
   1   2   3   4   5   6   ⑦   8   9   10

3. **How well is the organization tapping the potential of all its employees?**

   Not tapping potential   Moderately tapping potential   Tapping most potential
   1   2   3   4   ⑤   6   7   8   9   10

4. **Rate the degree to which you are treated with respect as a professional here.**

   Low   Average   High
   1   ②   3   4   5   6   7   8   9   10

5. **Rate the degree to which you know what is expected of you in your job.**

   Expectations not clear   Expectations moderately clear   Expectations very clear
   1   2   ③   4   5   6   7   8   9   10

6. **How much feedback, formal or informal, do you get from your manager?**

   Not enough feedback   Moderate feedback   Enough feedback
   1   ②   3   4   5   6   7   8   9   10

Organizational Climate Survey—Worksheet (continued)

7. **How useful is the feedback in developing your job performance?**

Not useful   Moderately useful   Very useful
1   (2)   3   4   5   6   7   8   9   10

8. **Rate the degree to which you think pay and promotions are linked to job performance.**

Not related at all   Moderately related   Directly related
1   2   (3)   4   5   6   7   8   9   10

9. **Who is more likely to get ahead here, someone who is competent or good at politics?**

Political person   Competent person
1   2   3   4   5   (6)   7   8   9   10

10. **Are mentors important for career advancement here?**   ☒ yes ☐ no

11. **Have you had what you would consider to be a mentor here?**   ☐ yes ☒ no

12. **Rate the degree to which the organization provides opportunities for all employees, regardless of race or gender.**

Opportunity not equal   Moderately equal   Opportunity very equal
1   2   (3)   4   5   6   7   8   9   10

13. **Rate the organization in creating an environment in which women can be successful.**

Not as good as others   Average   Better than others
1   2   (3)   4   5   6   7   8   9   10

14. **Rate the organization in creating an environment in which people of color can be successful.**

Not as good as others   Average   Better than others
1   2   3   4   (5)   6   7   8   9   10

15. **Have you ever witnessed or heard about behaviors exhibiting bias here? (jokes, non-inclusive language, double standards, exclusion in meetings, harassment, etc.)**

☒ yes ☐ no

16. **Is it acceptable to discuss issues of bias with your supervisor?**   ☐ yes ☒ no

17. **Rate the degree of teamwork experienced in your department.**

Low   Average   High
1   2   (3)   4   5   6   7   8   9   10

18. **Rate the degree of openness in communication within your department.**

Low   Average   High
1   (2)   3   4   5   6   7   8   9   10

19. **Rate the overall quality of supervision you have had here.**

Poor   Average   Excellent
(1)   2   3   4   5   6   7   8   9   10

20. **Rate overall the quality of work life here.**

Low   Average   High
1   2   (3)   4   5   6   7   8   9   10

Organizational Reasons to Value Diversity

Purpose

The purpose of the following worksheet is to determine an organization's reasons for undertaking a diversity effort, provide answers to the question "why?", as well as to identify benefits which relate to the bottom-line—making diversity more than just a "nice-to-have" initiative. This can be used as part of the introductory diversity presentation, or as a tool for working with senior management on an overall diversity effort.

Time

- 5 minutes to fill out, 5 minutes to discuss

Materials

- Handout, Organizational Reasons to Value Diversity (page 248) and pencils

---

Procedure

Prior to beginning the diversity effort, ask senior management to rate the importance of each reason for the organization in undertaking a diversity effort. Ask them to think of the positive impact diversity might have in contributing to the organization's business goals for each item.

The results can be used to increase the organization's momentum and commitment to the diversity effort, and to remind people that this is a bottom-line issue which is only going to become more important in years to come. In particular, they should be incorporated into the Our Organization's Value for Diversity handout on page 169. The results can also be discussed during workshops, to help participants understand which factors are most crucial in causing the organization to want an increased value for diversity.

Debrief

Ask participants the following questions:

- Which reasons do you think are most important?

- Are there any reasons missing?

- What would happen to the organization if we didn't value diversity?

Conclude by saying that the organization has many important reasons to value diversity. Diversity is more than just "nice-to-have"; it is a bottom-line business issue which will be increasingly important for the organization in years to come.

Organizational Reasons to Value Diversity—Worksheet

Rate below the importance of each item to this organization in creating a successful diversity effort. How important are these factors to creating a successful diversity effort in this organization?

How important is it for this organization to:	Level of Importance		
	Not very	Somewhat	Very
1. Adapt to population statistics of Workforce 2000	1 2	3 4	5
2. Better understand our customers	1 2	3 4	5
3. Compete for the best employees	1 2	3 4	5
4. Foster innovation and well-rounded perspectives on decisions	1 2	3 4	5
5. Support organizational goals of valuing diversity	1 2	3 4	5
6. Understand other organization's cultures during mergers	1 2	3 4	5
7. Reduce legal or affirmative action problems	1 2	3 4	5
8. Reduce conflict among diverse groups of employees	1 2	3 4	5
9. Support our organization's values	1 2	3 4	5
10. Do the right thing	1 2	3 4	5
11. (Other) _____	1 2	3 4	5
12. (Other) _____	1 2	3 4	5

Organization Diversity Strategies

Purpose   The following worksheet determines to what degree an organization is implementing the strategies needed for a successful diversity effort. It provides answers to the question "how?" which go beyond education and training and addresses structural and organizational issues which can support or hinder a diversity effort. This can be used as a tool for working with senior management to create a total strategy for valuing diversity. The results can be used as part of the introductory diversity presentation, to inform employees of what the organization is doing overall to value diversity.

Time   • 5 minutes to fill out, 5 minutes to discuss

Materials   • Handout, Organization Diversity Strategies (page 250) and pencils

---

Procedure   Prior to beginning the diversity effort, ask senior management to rank the organization's current level of effectiveness in implementing each diversity strategy. Tabulate the results to determine the organization's current level of effectiveness and areas for improvement in implementing a total diversity strategy. The results can also be compared to the results from the Organization Climate Survey (page 245) to determine greatest areas of need.

The results can also be discussed during workshops, to help participants understand what the organization is doing, in addition to training, to support the diversity effort. In particular, they should be incorporated into the handout, Our Organization's Value for Diversity (page 169).

Debrief   Ask participants the following questions:

• After seeing these, how committed do you think the organization is to valuing diversity?

• What are we doing right?

• What else do we need to do?

Conclude by saying that the organization has demonstrated commitment to valuing diversity in many ways in addition to training.

Organization Diversity Strategies—Worksheet

Rate the degree to which the organization is implementing the elements of a comprehensive diversity strategy. For each statement, circle the number that best applies.

Degree of Implementation:	Low	Medium	High

Recruiting

We have a process for hiring and promoting people based on competence, without projecting stereotypes of a person's diversity. We make a concerted effort to include a variety of candidates in selection decisions.

1   2   3   4   5

Performance management

We have a performance management process which includes diversity as a dimension on which people receive feedback on their behavior.

1   2   3   4   5

Compensation

We regularly conduct reviews of compensation to ensure that it is equal across racial and gender differences for equivalent jobs.

1   2   3   4   5

Benefits

We regularly provide flexible benefits which cater to the needs of nontraditional employees, such as dual-career parents, single parents, single people without children, and unmarried people with domestic partners.

1   2   3   4   5

Communication

We reinforce diversity as an integral part of this organization by including the topic in organizational communications, such as speeches, newsletters, memos, e-mail, voice mail, bulletin boards, etc.

1   2   3   4   5

Events

We provide people with the opportunity to educate each other and to celebrate their diversity through events such as educational lunches, guest speakers, exhibits, etc.

1   2   3   4   5

Training and education

All employees, including senior management, are required to participate in diversity workshops. A senior managers introduces every workshop to show support.

1   2   3   4   5

(Other) _____ 1   2   3   4   5

(Other) _____ 1   2   3   4   5

Diversity Statistics

Purpose
The purpose of this quiz is to make participants aware of current demographic trends in the U.S. which vividly demonstrate the reality of diversity and the end of the homogeneous workplace. It also can act as an "eye-opener" to get people's attention and interest in the subject. Often, people think they know the answers and are surprised to find how many they get wrong.

Time
Materials
- 15 minutes
- Handouts, Diversity Statistics Quiz (page 252) and Diversity Statistics Quiz Answers (page 255)
- Overhead, Diversity Statistics Quiz Answers (page 276)

Procedure
Either before the workshop, or during the activity, ask participants to complete the quiz. When they are finished, reveal the answers and have them score themselves and determine their category. Tell them they will not have to reveal their scores. This information is for their use only in determining how aware they are of their environment and current trends.

Debrief
Ask the following questions:
- How did you do? Did you know as much about your environment as you thought you did?
- Are there any comments or questions on any of these statistics?
- How do you think these trends will change the products and services we offer?
- How will the workplace be different because of these trends?
- How will your job be different?

Tell participants that most of the statistics came from the Workforce 2000 report, or from other government studies. Review a few pertinent items from the quiz. For example, say:

> "In question 1, we can see that the workplace was created in ways that reflected the needs of the people who were originally in it. This is natural and no one is to blame. The problem is that the workplace has become outdated for the people who are in it now."

See the following answer sheet for other interesting items to highlight.

Summarize by saying that it is normal for people to score poorly on this quiz. It is just a demonstration that things have changed without us noticing. We need to embrace this new reality, and find ways of addressing diversity as an advantage which can enrich our workplaces and help us understand our customers better.

Diversity Statistics Quiz

How up-to-date are you on the trends shaping the American population? Circle your best guess for each question. We'll discuss the correct answers in the workshop.

1. The average worker in 1965 was a 29-year-old white male who was married, had children, and had fewer than 12 years of education.

    a. True
    b. False

2. The U.S. Dept. of Labor predicts that, by the year 2000, what percentage of new entrants to the workforce will be women and minorities, and what percentage will be white males?

    a. 50% women and minorities/50% white males
    b. 65% women and minorities/35% white males
    c. 85% women and minorities/15% white males

3. In 1991, what percentage of the U.S. workforce were men?

    a. 48%
    b. 56%
    c. 67%

4. According to the U.S. Department of Labor, in 1989 what percent of working adults were white women, and what percent of the workforce were minorities?

    a. 20% white women/8% minorities
    b. 35% white women/15% minorities
    c. 45% white women/20% minorities

5. In a survey by Korn/Ferry International of 1,362 Fortune 500 executives, what percentage were women, and what percentage were racial minorities?

    a. 2% women/1% racial minorities
    b. 10% women/5% racial minorities
    c. 20% women/10% racial minorities

6. In 1990, using the official definition, 33.6 million people were classified as poor. Most poor people in the U.S. were:

    a. white
    b. black
    c. Hispanic

7. The fastest growing race in America is people of Asian decent. True/False

8. According to the U.S. Census Bureau, black people are currently the largest racial minority group in the U.S. What share of the population is African-American?

    a. 1 in 20
    b. 1 in 8
    c. 1 in 4

Diversity Statistics Quiz (continued)

9. The U.S. Census Bureau estimates that Hispanics will exceed African-Americans as America's largest racial minority in what year?

   a. 2000
   b. 2010
   c. 2020

10. By the year 2000, what ratio of Americans will be Black, Hispanic, or Asian?

    a. 1 in 15
    b. 1 in 10
    c. 1 in 4

11. How many languages are currently estimated to be spoken in California?

    a. 20
    b. 50
    c. 80

12. High divorce rates and increasing numbers of unmarried mothers contribute to the growing number of children living with single parents, and these families are disproportionately poor. What share of American children live in single-parent families?

    a. 1 in 10
    b. 1 in 4
    c. 1 in 2

13. What percentage of U.S. families now have the traditional "father working, mother at home, with 2.4 children" scenario?

    a. 10%
    b. 20%
    c. 40%

14. The American Demographics research group predicts that by the year 2000, what percentage of U.S. households headed by 35- to 54-year-olds will have male homemakers?

    a. 5%
    b. 15%
    c. 37%

15. How many Americans between the ages of 16 and 24 are high-school drop outs?

    a. 301 in 20
    b. 1 in 10

16. What is the estimated number of American adults who are gay or lesbian?

    a. 1 in 20
    b. 1 in 10
    c. 1 in 5

Diversity Statistics Quiz (continued)

17. By the year 2000, as many Americans will be over age 75 as will be under age 5.

    a. True
    b. False

18. The U.S. Census Bureau predicts that, by the year 2000, the average worker will be how old?

    a. 25
    b. 32
    c. 40

19. What is the largest of all minority groups in America?

    a. blacks
    b. gays
    c. people with disabilities

20. When Schick Razors was asked by *The Wall Street Journal* about their advertising which emphasizes multicultural faces and personalities, they stated that:

    a. "We had a drop in sales to the older white male customer base."
    b. "We saw immediate sales growth."
    c. "We had a small increase in sales from minority members."

21. Racial minority shoppers spent how much on U.S. goods in 1992?

    a. $20 billion
    b. $200 billion
    c. $600 billion

22. New York City—the U.S.'s largest city—is one of the ten largest cities in the world.

    a. True
    b. False

Diversity Statistics Quiz—Answers

Answers are highlighted in bold type. Interesting statistical information you may wish to highlight is added to the bottom of a few questions.

1. The average worker in 1965 was a 29-year-old white male who was married, had children, and had fewer than 12 years of education.
   a. **True**
   b. False

2. The U.S. Dept. of Labor predicts that, by the year 2000, what percentage of new entrants to the workforce will be women and minorities, and what percentage will be white males?
   a. 50%/50%
   b. 65%/35%
   c. **85%/15%**

3. In 1991, what percentage of the U.S. workforce were men?
   a. **48%**
   b. 56%
   c. 67%

4. According to the U.S. Department of Labor, in 1989 what percent of working adults were white women, and what percent of the workforce were minorities?
   a. 20%/8%
   b. 35%/15%
   c. **45%/20%**

5. In a survey by Korn/Ferry International of 1,362 Fortune 500 executives, what percentage were women, and what percentage were racial minorities?
   a. **2%/1%**
   b. 10%/5%
   c. 20%/10%

6. In 1990, using the official definition, 33.6 million people were classified as poor. Most poor people in the U.S. were:
   a. **white**
   b. black
   c. Hispanic

7. The fastest growing race in America is people of Asian decent.
   a. True
   b. **False (Is Hispanics)**

8. According to the U.S. Census Bureau, black people are currently the largest racial minority group in the U.S. What share of the population is African-American?
   a. 1 in 20
   b. **1 in 8**
   c. 1 in 4

Diversity Statistics Quiz—Answers (continued)

9. The U.S. Census Bureau estimates that Hispanics will exceed African-Americans as America's largest racial minority in what year?
   a. 2000
   b. 2010
   c. 2020

10. By the year 2000, what ratio of Americans will be Black, Hispanic, or Asian?
    a. 1 in 15
    b. 1 in 10
    c. 1 in 4

11. How many languages are currently estimated to be spoken in California?
    a. 20
    b. 50
    c. 80

12. High divorce rates and increasing numbers of unmarried mothers contribute to the growing number of children living with single parents, and these families are disproportionately poor. What share of American children live in single-parent families?
    a. 1 in 10
    b. 1 in 4
    c. 1 in 2

13. What percentage of U.S. families now have the traditional "father working, mother at home, with 2.4 children" scenario?
    a. 10%
    b. 20%
    c. 40%

14. The American Demographics research group predicts that by the year 2000, what percentage of U.S. households headed by 35- to 54-year-olds will have male homemakers?
    a. 5%
    b. 15%
    c. 37%

15. How many Americans between the ages of 16 and 24 are high-school drop outs?
    a. in 30
    b. 1 in 20
    c. 1 in 10

16. What is the estimated number of American adults who are gay or lesbian?
    a. 1 in 20
    b. 1 in 10
    c. 1 in 5

Diversity Statistics Quiz—Answers (continued)

17. By the year 2000, as many Americans will be over age 75 as will be under age 5.
    a. **True**
    b. False

18. The U.S. Census Bureau predicts that, by the year 2000, the average worker will be how old?
    a. 25
    b. 32
    c. **40**

19. What is the largest of all minority groups in America?
    a. blacks
    b. gays
    c. **people with disabilities (includes people with HIV and AIDS, and many older people).**

20. When Schick Razors was asked by *The Wall Street Journal* about their advertising which emphasizes multicultural faces and personalities, they stated that:
    a. "We had a drop in sales to the older white male customer base."
    b. **"We saw immediate sales growth."**
    c. "We had a small increase in sales from minority members."

21. Racial minority shoppers spent how much on U.S. goods in 1992?
    a. $20 billion
    b. $200 billion
    c. **$600 billion**

22. New York City—the U.S.'s largest city—is one of the ten largest cities in the world.
    a. True
    b. **False**

1. Mexico City	Mexico	12,900,000
2. Cairo	Egypt	12,500,000
3. Shanghai	China	11,900,000
4. Sao Paulo	Brazil	10,100,000
5. Seoul	S. Korea	9,600,000
6. Beijing	China	9,300,000
7. Moscow	Russia	8,700,000
8. Tokyo	Japan	8,400,000
9. Tinjin	China	7,800,000
10. Jakarta	Indonesia	7,600,000
11. New York	U.S.A.	7,300,000

Valuing Diversity Self-Assessment

Purpose

The purpose of this assessment is to give people the opportunity to reflect on their own behaviors in valuing diversity and create goals for development. It can also be used by others to assess the workshop participants, thereby providing 360-degree feedback.

Time

- 5 to 10 minutes

Materials

- Assessment, Valuing Diversity Self-Assessment (page 259)

- Handout, Valuing Diversity Scoring (page 261)

- Pencils

Procedure

Give the assessment to participants either before the workshop, or during the activity. Ask them to rate themselves honestly and openly. They will not be required to disclose their scores unless they want to. The assessment is for their own use only.

Debrief

Ask participants the following questions:

- What do each of the scoring categories mean to you?

- In which category do you think the organization would like everyone to score?

- How can you use this information in your efforts to better value diversity?

Conclude by saying that, while most people fall in the Traditional or Neutral categories, the company is doing this diversity training to encourage more people to be Change Agents. People may want to create a diversity goal for themselves based on any items for which they scored themselves lower than they would like.

Valuing Diversity Self-Assessment—Worksheet

Rate yourself openly and honestly on a scale of 1 to 5 for each item.

	Rarely	Sometimes		Always
1. I understand the company's diversity goals.	1	2	3	4	5
2. I regularly assess my strengths and weaknesses in the area of diversity, and I consciously try to improve myself.	1	2	3	4	5
3. I'm always asking questions. I'm curious about new things and people.	1	2	3	4	5
4. When I don't understand what someone says, I ask for clarification.	1	2	3	4	5
5. I'm committed to respecting all co-workers, customers, and vendors.	1	2	3	4	5
6. I work willingly and cooperatively with people different from me.	1	2	3	4	5
7. I recognize how bonding with my own group may exclude, or be perceived as excluding others.	1	2	3	4	5
8. I can communicate with and influence people who are different from me in positive ways.	1	2	3	4	5
9. I'm interested in the ideas of people who don't think as I do, and I respect their opinions even when I disagree.	1	2	3	4	5
10. Some of my friends are different from me in age, race, background, etc.	1	2	3	4	5
11. I recognize I'm a product of my background; my way isn't the only way.	1	2	3	4	5
12. I'm aware of my prejudices and consciously try to control my assumptions about people.	1	2	3	4	5
13. I try to help others understand my differences.	1	2	3	4	5
14. I work to make sure that people who are different from me are heard and are respected.	1	2	3	4	5

Valuing Diversity Self-Assessment—Worksheet (continued)

	Rarely	Sometimes			Always
15. I help others succeed by sharing unwritten rules and showing them how to function better.	1	2	3	4	5
16. I apologize when I've offended someone.	1	2	3	4	5
17. I resist the temptation to make another group the scapegoat when something goes wrong.	1	2	3	4	5
18. I think of the impact of my comments and actions before I speak or act.	1	2	3	4	5
19. I refrain from repeating rumors that reinforce prejudice or bias.	1	2	3	4	5
20. I recognize and avoid using language that reinforces stereotypes.	1	2	3	4	5
21. I include people different from me in informal networks and events.	1	2	3	4	5
22. I believe and convey that nontraditional employees are as skilled and competent as others.	1	2	3	4	5
23. I get to know people as individuals who are different from me.	1	2	3	4	5
24. I turn over responsibility to people who are different from me as often as I do to people who are like me.	1	2	3	4	5
25. I disregard physical characteristics when interacting with others and when making decisions about competence or ability.	1	2	3	4	5
26. I avoid generalizing the behaviors or attitudes of one individual to an entire group. (e.g., "All men are . . .," "All Jewish people are . . .," etc.)	1	2	3	4	5
27. I say "I think that's inappropriate" when I think someone is making a derogatory comment or joke.	1	2	3	4	5
28. I recognize that others may stereotype me, and I try to overcome incorrect assumptions that they may make.	1	2	3	4	5

Total by column   _____

Total score   _____

Valuing Diversity Self-Assessment—Scoring

Unaware	Traditional	Neutral	Change Agent	Rebel
0-39	40-69	70-99	100-129	130-140

Unaware
(0 to 39)

Unaware people don't realize they exhibit biased behavior. They may offend others without being aware of it. They may accept stereotypes as facts. They may even unknowingly be committing illegal acts. An unaware person's scores can fall in any category because an unaware person might answer "always" or "frequently" when in reality he or she just does not comprehend biased behavior. Because unaware people "don't know what they don't know," the only accurate indicator is feedback from others.

Traditional
(40 to 69)

Traditionals are aware of their prejudices, and that their behavior may offend some people. Nevertheless, they continue with derogatory jokes, comments, and actions and act as though laws and the organization's values don't apply to them. If you fall in this category, not only is it likely that your behavior is damaging workplace productivity, but it could bring legal implications as well. People in this category often use bias in employment decisions and treatment of co-workers—which is illegal. Look at the questions you marked lowest. You might want to create goals which will help you break these habits.

Neutral
(70 to 99)

People in this category are aware of biases in themselves and others. They are working to overcome their own prejudices, but are reluctant to address inappropriate behavior by others. They avoid risk by saying nothing, and this behavior is often perceived as agreement. If you fall into this category, look at the questions that you marked the lowest. You may want to create goals to improve those areas. You can also work on ways to become more proactive with regard to others' biases.

Change agent
(100 to 129)

These people are aware of biases in themselves and others, and realize the negative impact of acting on those biases. They're willing to take action when they encounter inappropriate words, behaviors, or structures. They relate to people in a way that values diversity. If you scored in this category, your greatest contribution is to help others value diversity more fully.

Rebel
(130 to 140)

Rebels are acutely aware of any behavior that seems to be prejudiced. They may even go too far and become involved in reverse discrimination. They have played an important part in helping nontraditional employees, but they pay a price. They may get a reputation that causes people to discount their views. If your score falls in this category, you may be a change agent but should also examine whether you are coming across too strongly or overreacting. Asking other people for honest feedback may help.

Managing Diversity Self-Assessment

Purpose

This assessment gives managers the opportunity to reflect on their own behaviors in managing diversity and to create goals for development. It can also be used as an "others" assessment for upward feedback.

Time

- 5 to 10 minutes

Materials

- Handout, Managing Diversity Self-Assessment (page 263)
- Pencils

Procedure

Give the assessment to participants either before the workshop or during the activity. Ask them to rate themselves honestly and openly. They will not be required to disclose their scores unless they want to. The assessment is for their own use only.

Debrief

Ask participants the following questions:

- How do you feel about your scores?
- How do you think the people who report to you would score you?
- How can you use this information in your efforts to better manage diversity?

Conclude by saying that, no matter how good a manager a person is, we all have room to improve in managing diversity. As role models, managers must set a positive example for others in the organization. Managers may want to create a diversity goal for themselves based on any items or categories for which they scored themselves lower than they would like.

Managing Diversity Self-Assessment—Worksheet

Rate yourself honestly on each item. Then total your column ratings and divide by the number of questions for your category rating. Then, create a goal to improve in your lowest scoring category.

Setting the Tone   **Rarely Sometimes Always**

1. I am a role model of valuing diversity to others.   1   2   3   4   5

2. I can communicate the value of diversity to others.   1   2   3   4   5

3. I have a strategy for learning about the values, differences, and priorities of each person who reports to me.   1   2   3   4   5

4. I acknowledge that people of different backgrounds can take different but equally effective approaches to their work, and I can avoid turning those differences into stereotypes.   1   2   3   4   5

5. I do all I can to create a work environment in which all employees and customers are respected and valued.   1   2   3   4   5

Total of Columns ____ **÷ 5 = Category Rating** _____ **Column Totals** _____

Employment Laws

6. I can interpret employment law and protect the company from instances of discrimination, harassment, and violations of equal opportunity.   1   2   3   4   5

Total of Columns ____ **÷ 5 = Category Rating** _____ **Column Totals** _____

Staffing

7. I make an effort to recruit, select, and promote nontraditional employees.   1   2   3   4   5

8. I disregard physical characteristics when interviewing or hiring.   1   2   3   4   5

9. I consider people who are different from me for all opportunities and promotions I have influence over.   1   2   3   4   5

Total of Columns ____ **÷ 5 = Category Rating** _____ **Column Totals** _____

Managing Diversity Self-Assessment—Worksheet (continued)

Performance Management	Rarely	Sometimes		Always	

10. I ensure that employees' job expectations are clear. 1 2 3 4 5

11. I recognize and correct biased or inappropriate words, humor,
gestures, and behaviors in others. 1 2 3 4 5

12. I know how to create a motivating environment for a variety of
people, both individually and as a group. 1 2 3 4 5

13. I take the biases of my own background into account when
reviewing employees' performance. 1 2 3 4 5

14. I give others honest feedback (both positive and negative) on job
performance in a manner appropriate to each individual's needs. 1 2 3 4 5

Total of Columns ___ **÷ 5 = Category Rating** ___ **Column Totals** _____

Empowering Employees

15. I turn over responsibility to people who are different from me as often
as I do to people who are like me. 1 2 3 4 5

16. I share unwritten rules with employees who are different from me. 1 2 3 4 5

17. I keep all people equally in the information loop. 1 2 3 4 5

Total of Columns ___ **÷ 5 = Category Rating** ___ **Column Totals** _____

Conflict Management

18. I can fairly mediate conflict between employees when one is similar
to me and one is different. 1 2 3 4 5

19. I foresee situations with potential problems involving differences,
and I take steps to prevent or defuse them. 1 2 3 4 5

Total of Columns ___ **÷ 5 = Category Rating** ___ **Column Totals** _____

Manager/Employee Interview

Purpose

This assessment gives managers a tool with which to understand employees' unique needs better—to implement "The Platinum Rule" and treat others as *they* want to be treated. Some questions can also be used as an anonymous "others" assessment for upward feedback. The questions can be used either one-on-one, in a team meeting, in both situations, or as an anonymous mail-in questionnaire.

Time

- Up to 60 minutes for a manager to use with one employee

Materials

- Handout, Manager/Employee Interview Questions (page 266)

- Pencils

Procedure

Hand out the questions to participants and have them review them.

Debrief

Ask participants the following questions:

- To what extent do you know the answers to these questions about your employees?

- How do you think the people who report to you would answer?

- How would it help you be an effective manager, if you knew the answers to these questions?

- How might you use these questions?

- What are some other ways managers can get to know their employees' unique needs?

Conclude by saying that this has been a useful tool for many managers in getting to know their employees' unique needs better, and in gaining feedback on their own ability to set a tone for diversity. Participants may choose to give employees the options of answering the questions individually, in a group, or as a written questionnaire.

Often, the answers provide managers with valuable insights. The questions also enable them to build open, positive relationships with employees.

Manager/Employee Interview—Questions

1. What do you want most from your job?

2. Under what conditions do you do your best work?

3. How would you like me to show recognition of your hard work?

4. How do you want to be rewarded?

5. How would you like to receive suggestions for improving your work?

6. What are your short-term career goals?

7. What are your longer-term career goals?

8. How can I help you reach your career goals?

9. In what ways do you think people in our department, including yourself, are different from one another?

10. How do these differences affect our working together as a team?

11. How do these differences affect interpersonal relationships on the job?

12. How do these differences affect our overall productivity?

13. What things am I doing that help the team work together?

14. What do I do that might hurt our productivity?

15. What suggestions do you have for me as a manager or team leader?

16. What biases do you perceive in me?

17. How do these biases manifest themselves in my actions?

18. What policies or procedures inhibit your best work?

Valuing Diversity Action Plan

Purpose

The purpose of the following worksheet is to close a session by relating employees' learning in the workshop to real-life goals and follow-through steps for valuing diversity.

Time

- 5 minutes

Materials

- Handout, Valuing Diversity Action Plan (page 268)

- Pencils

Procedure

Tell participants this is the most important part of the workshop, because it is what they do afterward that really matters in creating an environment that values diversity. Tell them the questions on the action plan are designed to stimulate their thinking, but the most important item is the one goal they will commit to acting on after the workshop. They should make the goal something realistic, at which they can succeed.

Encourage participants to use ideas they learned in the workshop, or improvement areas from their assessments, as their goals. Hand out the Valuing Diversity Action Plan and have participants complete them. Tell them that when they're finished, the group will take a few minutes for people who would like to share their goals.

Debrief

Ask participants the following questions:

- Who would like to share your goal?

- Do you think your goal is realistic and achievable?

Conclude by saying that their actions are what will create an environment for valuing diversity. Valuing diversity benefits *everyone*, because it liberates us to be appreciated for who we really are. If every person in this room follows through on his or her goal, we will all benefit from a better work environment, as well as greater productivity and teamwork which will have a positive impact on the organization's bottom line. One person's actions *can* make a difference. Conclude by asking for their commitment.

Valuing Diversity Action Plan—Worksheet

My most important diversity goal, which I commit to working toward, is:

_____

_____

_____

_____

Benefits I will gain from valuing diversity:

_____

_____

_____

_____

Things about myself that I will communicate to help others work more productively with me:

_____

_____

_____

_____

Perceptions about people who are different from me that I will work to change:

_____

_____

_____

_____

Ways I will contribute to creating an environment that values diversity:

_____

_____

_____

_____

Resources I will use to continue to learn about diversity:

_____

_____

_____

_____

Managing Diversity Action Plan

Purpose   This assessment is used to close a session by relating managers'
                     learning in the workshop to real-life goals and follow-through steps
                     for managing diversity.

Time   • 5 minutes

Materials   • Handout, Managing Diversity Action Plan

                     • Pencils

Procedure   Tell participants this is the most important part of the workshop,
                     because it is what they do afterward that really matters in creating
                     an environment that values diversity. Tell them the questions on the
                     action plan are designed to stimulate their thinking, but the most
                     important item is the one goal they will commit to acting on after
                     the workshop. They should make the goal something realistic, at
                     which they can succeed.

   Encourage participants to use ideas they learned in the workshop,
                     or improvement areas from their assessments, as their goals. Hand
                     out the Managing Diversity Action Plan and have participants com-
                     plete them. Tell them that when they're finished, the group will
                     take a few minutes for people who would like to share their goals.

Debrief   Ask participants the following questions:

                     • Who would like to share your goal?

                     • Do you think your goal is realistic and achievable?

   Conclude by saying that their actions are what will create an envi-
                     ronment for valuing diversity. As managers their role is especially
                     important because others look to them as role models. If every
                     manager in this room follows through on his or her goal, everyone
                     will benefit from a better work environment, as well as achieve
                     greater productivity and teamwork. This will have a positive
                     impact on the organization's bottom line. One person's actions *can*
                     make a difference. Conclude by asking for their commitment.

Managing Diversity Action Plan—Worksheet

My most important diversity goal, which I commit to working toward, is:

_____

_____

_____

_____

Benefits I will gain from managing diversity:

_____

_____

_____

_____

Perceptions about managing diversity that I will make an effort to change:

_____

_____

_____

_____

Skills for managing diversity that I will work to develop in myself:

_____

_____

_____

_____

Ways I will create an environment that values diversity in my department:

_____

_____

_____

_____

Ways I can be a change agent in making sure the structures of the organization value diversity:

_____

_____

_____

_____

Resources I will use to continue to learn about managing diversity:

_____

_____

_____

_____

Diversity Workshop Reaction

Purpose

This worksheet is used to gather information from participants for enhancements to the program (and the overall diversity effort) which can be made for future sessions. To gain feedback for the trainer on his or her strengths and areas for development.

Time

- 5 minutes

Materials

- Handout, Diversity Workshop Reaction Sheet (page 272)

- Pencils

Procedure

As the last activity of the workshop, hand out the Diversity Workshop Reaction Sheets and ask participants to fill them out candidly. Ask them to leave them in an envelope or on a chair at the back of the room as they leave. Use results to gain insights into improving the program and the trainer's skills. Also, they can be used to gauge people's perceptions of the organization's commitment to diversity overall (as evidenced in questions 12 and 13).

Diversity Workshop Reaction—Worksheet

Rate your level of agreement or disagreement with the following statements. Please answer candidly and write your general comments at the bottom. Your responses are anonymous and will help us to improve the workshop for future participants.

	Disagree		Neutral		Agree
1. The concepts will help to better manage the new workforce.	1	2	3	4	5
2. Written materials were informative and well-written.	1	2	3	4	5
3. The audiovisual materials helped clarify the subject.	1	2	3	4	5
4. The trainer established an environment where people felt free to openly share their views.	1	2	3	4	5
5. The trainer understood the subject and workshop content.	1	2	3	4	5
6. The trainer encouraged people to participate.	1	2	3	4	5
7. I felt involved in the workshop.	1	2	3	4	5
8. The trainer helped me to relate ideas to my own experience.	1	2	3	4	5
9. I understood the purpose of activities and how to complete them.	1	2	3	4	5
10. The pace of the workshop was productive.	1	2	3	4	5
11. I was enthusiastic about the workshop prior to attending.	1	2	3	4	5
12. My manager is a positive role model of valuing diversity.	1	2	3	4	5
13. I believe this organization is committed to valuing diversity.	1	2	3	4	5
14. I am going to put into action what I learned in this session.	1	2	3	4	5

15. The most valuable part was:

_____

_____

_____

16. The least valuable part was:

_____

_____

_____

17. Comments (use back also):

_____

_____

_____

Chapter Nine:

Overhead Transparencies

This section of the sourcebook contains the overheads suggested for the workshops in Chapters 3, 4, and 5. You can also use them for your own diversity workshop designs. They are the key visual images that enhance the written, oral, and experiential methods with which trainers help people learn about diversity.

HOW TO USE THE OVERHEADS

You can use the overheads in a variety of ways:

- Photocopy them onto transparencies as overheads.

- Photocopy them onto paper as handouts.

- Transcribe them onto flipcharts for use as visuals (if an overhead projector is not available.)

- The overheads are all ready to be used "as is."

 You will need to draw in the learning curves on the Learning Curve overhead (page 284) as you describe it to participants. Complete descriptions of how to do this can be found in Chapters 3 and 4. A filled-in example of the overhead is provided on page 285 in this chapter.

DIVERSITY DEFINED

Diversity is the mosaic of people who bring a variety of backgrounds, styles, perspectives, values, and beliefs as assets to the groups and organizations with which they interact.

PRIMARY AND SECONDARY DIMENSIONS OF DIVERSITY

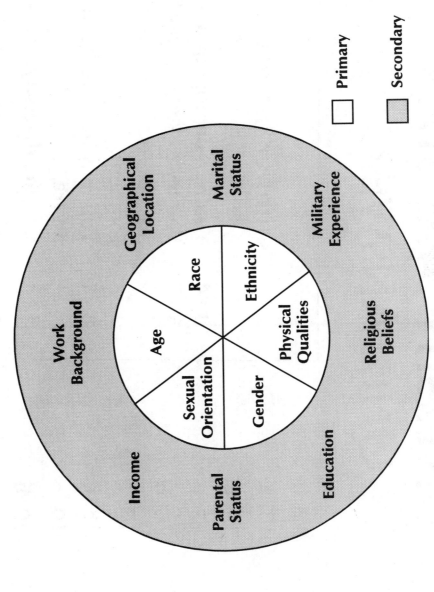

Primary

Secondary

Loden and Rosener, *Workforce America!* 1991

DIVERSITY STATISTICS QUIZ ANSWERS

1. True
2. c
3. a
4. c
5. a
6. a
7. False
8. b
9. a
10. c
11. c

12. b
13. a
14. c
15. c
16. b
17. True
18. c
19. c
20. b
21. c
22. False

Number Incorrect

0 - 4	You're a demographics whiz.
5 - 7	You try to keep current and are observant of your environment.
8 - 11	You may need to be more aware.
12 +	Call the diversity awareness patrol!

WORKPLACE TRENDS AND STATISTICS

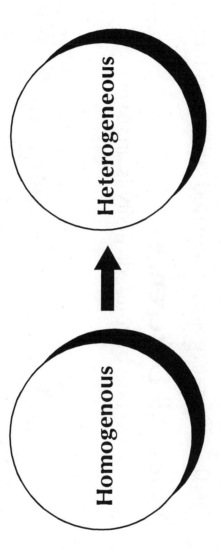

Homogenous → Heterogeneous

- Equal balance of men and women

- ↘ % whites, ↗ % people of color

- 85% new entrants will be women, people of color

- Aging of the workforce

- Bigger gaps in education

- Shortage of new entrants

- High competition for best employees

277

APPROACHES TO DIVERSITY

- ## The Golden Rule
  1960s, assimilation, "stop treating people badly"

- ## Right the Wrongs
  1970s, affirmative action, created "us versus them"

- ## Value All Differences
  Year 2000 and beyond, diversity is an asset

PERCEPTIONS AND STEREOTYPES

Perceptions

- Raised in homogeneous communities.
- Gravitate toward people like us.
- Uncomfortable with differences we don't understand.
- Screen out evidence which contradicts existing perceptions.

Stereotypes

- Fixed generalizations about people in certain groups.
- Judgements don't take into account the here and now.

Prejudice

- Seeing differences as weaknesses.

Ethnocentrism

- One's own group is superior to all others.

Collusion Defined

Collusion is cooperation with others, knowingly or unknowingly, to reinforce stereotypical attitudes, prevailing behaviors, and norms.

Types of collusion include:

- Silence
- Denial
- Active Participation

THE PLATINUM RULE

Treat others as *they* want to be treated.

How Managers Set a Tone for Valuing Diversity

- Be a Role Model

- Use the Platinum Rule

- Project Positive Self-Fulfilling Prophecies

CHANGES IN VIEWPOINT ON DIVERSITY

Old View

- Affirmative Action
- "Being nice to minorities"
- Race/gender differences
- Dominant culture's bias
- Learn about cultures
- Burden
- Golden Rule
- Melting pot

Modern View

- Valuing diversity
- Makes good business sense
- Infinite number of differences/similarities
- We all have biases
- Learn about people as individuals
- Asset
- Platinum Rule
- Mosaic

LEARNING CURVE

Competence

With
Training/Education

Training

Mastery

Without
Training/Education

On-the-Job
Practice

Time

284

Learning Curve

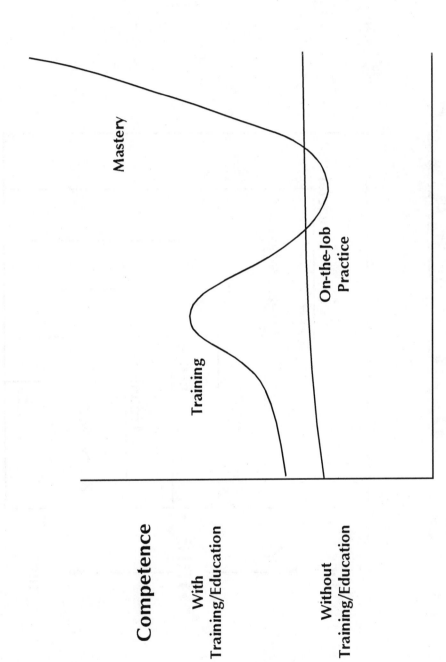

Competence

With Training/Education

Without Training/Education

Mastery

Training

On-the-Job Practice

Time

285

STAGES OF CHANGE

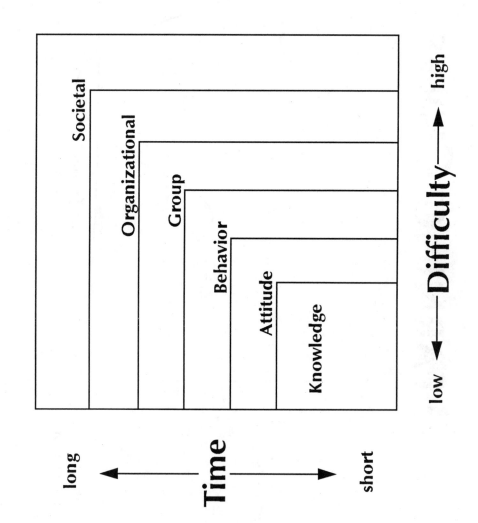

286

Recommended Reading

As previously suggested, it is helpful to read this workbook several times as you prepare to facilitate a workshop. The handouts are especially useful in gaining an understanding of the topic. You can even memorize them for use in presentation and discussion segments. You will also benefit from reviewing some additional resources on diversity. Following is an annotated bibliography of the author's "top ten" most highly recommended resources.

Newsletter

Managing Diversity Newsletter, Jamestown Area Labor Management Committee. Phone: 716-665-3654.

This newsletter is a concise overview of current trends and issues regarding diversity. Each issue includes a question and answer segment, as well as a review of a new resource on diversity.

Articles

Carnevale, T., and S. Stone. "Diversity Beyond the Golden Rule." *Training & Development,* October 1994, 22–39. Phone: 703-683-8100.

This is an excellent, rich article which provides a comprehensive overview of every conceivable aspect of diversity training as it has evolved over the years. In many ways, it is a written documentary on the field of diversity. It also compares and contrasts various methods and approaches which have been used. You will benefit greatly from reading it as one of your first introductions to the topic.

Esty, K. "Diversity is Good for Business." *Executive Excellence,* January 1988, 5–6.

This short article summarizes research which has been done on the business benefits of diversity. It is an excellent resource for helping people to see how diversity relates to the bottom line. You can also use it as a handout or supplemental mailing to managers to demonstrate the positive impact of valuing diversity.

Thomas, R. "From Affirmative Action to Affirming Diversity." *Harvard Business Review,* March / April 1990, 107–117. Phone: 617-495-6800.

This classic article is an outstanding primer on the philosophical view of diversity as an issue which extends beyond affirmative action. It has a strong emphasis on managing diversity, and infrastructural issues which need to be addressed for a successful diversity effort. It also serves as a summary of the author's 1991 book *Beyond Race and Gender* (published by Amacom) which is also excellent and includes many case study examples of his diversity work with clients.

Books

Loden, M., and J. Rosener. *Workforce America!* Homewood, IL: Business One Irwin, 1991.

This book, one of the first to be published on diversity, provides a useful overview of the facts and figures which started the movement. It is easy to understand and is the source of the primary and secondary dimensions of diversity concept used extensively in this sourcebook.

Rasmussen, T. "Diversity Effort Succeeds Based on Needs Assessment Findings." *In Action: Conducting Needs Assessment.* Alexandria, VA: American Society for Training and Development.

The author of the *ASTD Trainer's Sourcebook: Diversity* has contributed a chapter to this book on diversity needs assessment, which can be a valuable resource on how to target and customize your own diversity effort.

Tannen, D. *You Just Don't Understand.* New York: Ballentine Books, 1990.

This book focuses specifically on differences in socialization and communication between men and women. It is a fascinating study which can explain the origins of many of our perceived differences.

Wigglesworth, D. *Resources for Workforce Diversity.* Fredonia, NY: H.R. Press, 1995. Phone: 716-672-4254.

This resource is a thorough and complete reference manual listing and describing most of the available resources on diversity. This comprehensive resource lists books, videos, games, simulations, and newsletters on diversity and has full descriptions of many. The author also writes a monthly column in the *Managing Diversity Newsletter* which reviews current releases of diversity resources.

Videos

"A Class Divided." PBS. 1985. Phone: 1-800-225-3959.

Although not required, this video is *highly* recommended for use in the one-day and half-day training designs in this book. In the author's experience, this has been an incredibly high-impact segment of the workshop for participants. It is a 1968 documentary set in the small, all-white farming community of Riceville, Iowa. A teacher creates a microcosm of society in her third-grade classroom by dividing the children into groups of blue-eyed and brown-eyed children. She then proceeds to create stereotypes and differences so they can experience alternately being "on the top" and "on the bottom." It is fascinating, and extremely revealing, for adults to observe how we do the same thing in more subtle ways.

The first 20 minutes are recommended for the one-day and half-day workshops, with the last 40 minutes being shown at lunch for the one-day workshop. The last 40 minutes features interviews with the grown children, relating the impact this exercise has had on them as adults. The video also documents how the teacher has done the same activity with groups of adults working in the prison system. The cost of this video is $200, and it is well worth the investment.

Do the Right Thing. Lee, S. 1991.

This Spike Lee production is a "slice of life" look at how diversity conflicts happen between people and at how difficult it is to "do the right thing" even when we want to. It is entertaining as well as thought provoking.

Index

About the Author

Tina Rasmussen is a group facilitator, consultant, and coach with more than fourteen years of training and organizational development experience helping executives, teams, and individuals develop humanistic business practices and financial strength. She has worked in many industries including high-tech, retail trade, financial services, and consumer products.

Her career mission is to help individuals and organizations create workplaces of increasingly self-actualizing values while providing value to their customers and achieving financial strength. Her specialty is working with leaders and organizations to translate their visions and goals into tangible plans, programs, and processes resulting in lasting, large-scale change. She is a strong proponent of experimental and self-directed learning and change methods.

Rasmussen's recent projects include a diversity effort for a Fortune 100 company, which was highlighted in ASTD's *Training & Development* magazine, ASTD Houston's *Torchbearer* magazine, and the *San Francisco Examiner*. Rasmussen describes this effort in her contribution to the ASTD book, *In Action: Conducting Needs Assessment*. Her other projects have included reengineering, customer satisfaction, technology change, leadership, and values-based vision linked with strategic planning.

An author and public speaker, Ms. Rasmussen has also been a newspaper reporter and columnist. She is a contributing author to the books *Leadership in a New Era* with Warren Bennis and *The Greenleaf Legacy* with Peter Senge. She also regularly speaks at conferences on HRD and humanistic business practices and is listed in *Who's Who of American Women*. Ms. Rasmussen has an M.A. in organizational development and is a Ph.D. candidate completing her doctor's dissertation on human and organizational systems at the Fielding Institute.

"KNOWLEDGE AND HUMAN POWER ARE SYNONYMOUS"

𝒦nowledge generates human performance. It doesn't take a famous quote or the picture of a tree to know that. But full potential requires the proper elements. Your professional growth can thrive, as a member of the American Society for Training and Development.

As an ASTD member you will get:

Information on the forefront of practice and technology

Access to colleagues around the world for idea-sharing

Opportunity to contribute to the advancement of your profession

through...international conferences and expositions...best practices...electronic resources and networking...benchmarking publications...personalized research assistance...and much more.

Join ASTD now...and become part of a worldwide association of nearly 58,000 leaders in the field of workplace learning and performance.

Call 703.683.8100. Or fax 703.683.1523
Mention Priority Code: MH5A
TDD: 703.683.4323

 ASTD
AMERICAN SOCIETY FOR TRAINING AND DEVELOPMENT

Delivering Performance in a Changing World